Secrets
of
Hannah

Donna K. Maltese

Secrets
of
Hannah

A Devotional for Women

BARBOUR
PUBLISHING

The Secrets of Hannah

Hannah was not a queen, a judge, or an ancestor of Jesus. She was just a woman, a wife, in deep despair. For she was barren, a condition that, in those days, made her worth—in her eyes and in the eyes of others—desperately low.

We find her story in the beginning of the first book of Samuel. And although her account is short, we learn many lessons that every woman, no matter what her condition, status, or situation, will find of value. For Hannah was not only a woman of much grace but one who knew the power of prayer and the importance of maintaining an intimate relationship with God. Within her story, we will see how a woman can secure the strength she needs to persevere in the present and find happiness in the future—all while enduring the seemingly unendurable.

The majority of the readings to follow will begin with a verse about Hannah from J. B. Steele's book *Sacred Poetical Paraphrases, and Miscellaneous Poems* and end with a scripture and prayer. We hope that as you peruse these pages, you will see how God can use the faith of an ordinary woman to demonstrate the power of prayer that rests in our hands—and how the results of those prayers can profoundly alter not just our personal story but the story of all God's people.

"I have poured out my
soul before the Lord."

1 Samuel 1:15 AMP

A Vicious Circle

Hannah's story takes place after the death of Joshua, the man God called to lead His people into the Promised Land. Once each tribe was settled in its designated territory, Joshua and those of his generation were "gathered to their ancestors. After them another generation rose up who did not know the LORD or the works He had done for Israel" (Judges 2:10 HCSB).

This new generation of Israelites served idols. Enraged at their cheating hearts, the God who had brought their ancestors out of Egypt raised up an adversary against them. After the Israelites had suffered and cried out to God for help, "the LORD raised up judges, who saved them" (Judges 2:16 HCSB). But once any particular judge died, God's people would soon fall back into their old ways and the cycle would begin all over again.

It's easy for us to shake our heads when reading about these Israelites. We wonder why they were trapped in this vicious circle in which they would anger God by worshipping false idols. God would then allow some disaster to befall them. The people would cry out for rescue, and God would send a judge to help them. For a while the people would enjoy a bit of peace. Then they'd get into trouble by not just ignoring God but replacing Him with a false idol! How could they not see what was happening and change their ways?

Yet don't we do the same? Are there not times when God seems further removed from us than ever, in fact, seems to have moved away—when in reality *we* are the ones who have moved, not He? Then, to fill the gap where God *should* be, we reach out for a substitute. We latch onto something—be it food, money, fashion, a man, or some other poor alternative—that will give us the love, comfort, support, and happiness we crave.

In our spiritual delusion, we think all is well. But then, when something comes our way to trouble us and our false idol proves unable to save us, we cry out to God who, in His never-ending compassion, rescues us. He pulls us in. He binds up our wounds, puts a healing balm upon our broken heart. For a while, relieved and grateful, we stay close to Him. Then, as the days go by, we drift away once again, attracted by something shiny, unique, or alluring in some other way. And before we know it, we're in trouble once more!

God doesn't want an off-again-on-again relationship with us. He wants us totally dedicated to Him. So instead of shaking our heads at the Israelites, let's take the splinter out of our own eyes and stick close to the one true God who has an endless supply of all we long for.

"God. . .is actually not far from each one of us."
ACTS 17:27 ESV

For You alone I reach, because You alone are the One I long for.

Worthy of Mention

Elkanah and his godly wife
In Ramah lived a peaceful life.

As we open up 1 Samuel, the beginning of Hannah's story, we meet a man named Elkanah with an almost once-upon-a-time introduction: "There was a certain man. . .named Elkanah" (1 Samuel 1:1 AMP). We're told he lives in Ramathaim-zophim, located in the hills of Ephraim. Yet he's from the tribe of Levi (1 Chronicles 6:25–28) and is identified as "son of Jeroham, son of Elihu, son of Tohu, son of Zuph" (1 Samuel 1:1 HCSB).

That's quite a few sons. Notice that no daughters, mothers, or wives are mentioned. That's because Hannah's story takes place in a heavily patriarchal society, at a time when women were treated somewhat like chattel, being second-class citizens with fewer rights and opportunities than their male counterparts. So if women were mentioned at all in a family tree, they were identified by their relationship to a man, that man being either a father, husband, brother, or son.

At its close, Jesus' own genealogy states that "all the generations from Abraham to David were 14 generations; and from David until the exile to Babylon, 14 generations; and from the exile to Babylon until the Messiah, 14 generations" (Matthew 1:17 HCSB). From the list of *forty-two* generations of men in Jesus' family that precedes this closing statement, only *five* women are mentioned: Tamar, Rahab, Ruth, Uriah's wife (a.k.a. Bathsheba), and Mary (1:3, 5, 6, 16). And who were these five women?

The first, the childless widow Tamar, posed as a prostitute, enticing her father-in-law, Judah, to lie with her, after which she became pregnant. Rahab actually *was* a prostitute before marrying Salmon and bearing Boaz. Ruth was a widowed Moabitess who married Boaz, providing a home for her former mother-in-law, Naomi. Bathsheba became caught up in adultery and later became a king's wife and mother. And Mary was a virgin who became pregnant before being touched by a human man. What a lineup! Yet each was, in her own way, a woman worthy of mention, a woman whose actions, courage, and determination changed the course of history.

Another such woman was Hannah, identified as Elkanah's godly wife. And it was the faith of Hannah, a seemingly ordinary woman, that changed the course of history.

You too may be such a woman as those few mentioned in the Bible. For when you let God into your life, when you allow Him to direct you, you find the courage and the perseverance to follow Him wherever He leads, regardless of your past missteps or present perils. Blessed beyond belief by your faith, you fix your eyes on Him alone each day, trusting in Him and His Word, seeing His promises fulfilled.

> *"Blessed is she who believed that there would be a*
> *fulfillment of what was spoken to her from the Lord."*
> Luke 1:45 esv

> *Lord, may I be a woman worthy of mention in*
> *Your book of life. In Jesus' name, amen.*

A Dark Cloud

But soon, too soon, a dark cloud throws
A shadow o'er their sweet repose.
No olive plants surround the board
Of Hannah and her loving lord.

Elkanah, a godly man, had married a godly woman named Hannah. Her name meant "grace"—just what Hannah was going to need as the years went on. . .and on. . .and on, and still no baby arrived. No little bundle appeared to demonstrate the viability of her womb, the proof of their love.

The couple's life was peaceful, quiet. A little too quiet, for there was no child's cry or lilt of laughter to break the silence of their house. This absence weighed heavily on Hannah's heart. For in her day, a woman's worth was tied to her ability to bear children.

We may wonder why God did not bless this loving couple with children—or why He delayed in blessing Abraham and Sarah, Isaac and Rebekah, Jacob and Rachel, Manoah and his (nameless) wife, the Shunamite and her husband, and Zechariah and Elizabeth. Or why any other couple then (or now) was bereft of the ability to bear a child.

Perhaps God needed to prepare the childless couples in some way, perhaps strengthen their faith by having them wait. Maybe He wanted the husband and wife to look to Him alone for solutions to their problems, answers to their prayers. But these are only conjectures, guesses as to the intentions of God, speculations of what His motives might have been. Even if we could ask God, face-to-face, why some are able to have children and others not, He may just turn to us and say, "What is that to you?" (John 21:22 ESV).

All we do know is that Hannah, like many women before and after her, was unable to have children. This meant she would be looked down upon by other women. She would be seen as worth less. As for personal consequences, Hannah's having no children meant there would be no one to look after her, to provide for her, if Elkanah died. She would have to go back to her father's house, or to the house of a brother or other close male relative—if they would be willing to take up such a burden as she.

Thank God today's women have more options available to them. More avenues to explore, more choices in the way they live their lives, as well as other alternatives to pursue if childbearing proves problematic.

Still, Hannah and Elkanah could find their delight in each other and have peace in their home. That is, until one of them decided not to wait for God but to find his own solution to their problem.

There was a certain man. . .named Elkanah.
1 SAMUEL 1:1 AMP

---

*Lord, help me to rejoice in the peace and love I already
have and to leave my list of desires in Your hands.*

God's Way Is Perfect

In evil hour Elkanah's house
Receives a second, youthful spouse. . .

Hannah and Elkanah's childlessness was like a shadow hanging over their bed. And Elkanah's solution to their problem would become an even bigger problem that neither he nor Hannah had bargained for.

Being a man of some prominence, Elkanah wanted a child, an heir, someone to carry on his family's name, wealth, and tradition. He wanted a branch on his family's tree. And since no heir was coming from Hannah's womb, he decided to take a second wife.

From the very beginning, of course, God's divine injunction was that one man was to cleave to one woman. "This is why a man leaves his father and mother and bonds with his wife, and they become one flesh" (Genesis 2:24 HCSB).

Jesus agreed, putting together two verses of Genesis (1:27; 5:2) and adding a statement of His own: "Have you never read that He who created them from the beginning *made them male and female, and said, 'For this reason a man shall leave his father and mother and shall be joined inseparably to his wife, and the two shall become one flesh'?* So they are no longer two, but one flesh. Therefore, what God has joined together, let no one separate" (Matthew 19:4–6 AMP).

Why else should one man have only one wife, and one woman have only one husband? Because having more than two people in one marriage spells nothing but trouble.

Consider what happened when an impatient, childless Sarah gave her maid Hagar to her husband, Abraham. It caused enmity not only between Sarah and Hagar but between their offspring, Sarah's Isaac (from whom the nation of Jews descended) and Hagar's Ishmael (from whom the nation of Arabs descended), an enmity that continues to this day!

Then there was the bitter rivalry between sisters Leah and Rachel. Not only did they compete to see who could provide their husband, Jacob, with the most children; they went so far as to give him their handmaids, Bilhah and Zilpah! And consider all the trouble Solomon's seven hundred wives caused, leading him to serve and worship idols rather than the one true God!

Marriage is hard enough without adding another member (or two or three) to the party. For when that happens, the wedding march quickly becomes a dirge as the marriage begins to die a slow and tumultuous death.

Too often our poorly conceived solutions to our problems result in our creating even more havoc in our lives. Better to leave all your great ideas and strategies in God's hands. For His plan is always and in all ways best!

> *God—His way is perfect; the word of the Lord is pure.*
> *He is a shield to all who take refuge in Him.*
> PSALM 18:30 HCSB

> *Lord, You are the holder of all wisdom. Help me*
> *look to You alone for all remedies to my ills.*

Choose for Yourself

Peninnah called, whose children rise,
The triumph of the Hebrew wives.

*E*lkanah, in an attempt to fill his home with children, takes a second wife. Why? Because even though it was against God's original intent, polygamy was accepted and prevalent among God's people, especially during those days when the judges ruled, when there was no king in Israel, and "every man did what was right in his own eyes" (Judges 21:25 AMP; see also Judges 17:6; 18:1; 19:1). And chaos prevailed among God's people.

The Hebrews were a nation set apart by God. They were supposed to follow the laws He'd laid down for them, to abide by His Word so they could reap the rewards of His blessings and promises. Instead, they opted to do what they wanted, regardless of what that might mean in their own lives and in the lives of others. About this passage, *Gill's Exposition of the Entire Bible* says:

> *Every man did that which was right in his own*
> *eyes; there being none to restrain him from it, or*
> *punish him for it; and this accounts for the many*
> *evil things related, as the idolatry of Micah and the*
> *Danites, the base usage of the Levite's concubine,*
> *the extreme rigour and severity with which the*
> *Israelites treated their brethren the Benjaminites,*
> *the slaughter of the inhabitants of Jabeshgilead,*
> *and the rape of the daughters of Shiloh.* *

Talk about chaos! Yet that's what reigns in our lives when we refuse to let God be the ruler of our hearts. When we do not submit to the authority of God's Word, our lives, homes, nation, and world become places of spiritual confusion and moral mayhem.

In 1 Samuel 8, Samuel's own sons were judges who "accepted bribes and perverted justice" (verse 3 NLT). So the leaders of the tribes of Israel said to Samuel, "Give us a king to judge us like all the other nations have" (verse 5 NLT). Although this request broke Samuel's heart, he went to God for guidance. And God, knowing how rebellious we are, told him the people weren't rejecting Samuel as their judge but God as their King. "Ever since I brought them from Egypt they have continually abandoned me and followed other gods. And now they are giving you the same treatment. Do as they ask" (verses 8–9 NLT).

When pleasing God is last on our list, we look for protection and security elsewhere, among our own kind, which ultimately leads to disappointment and heartache. Every day you can choose to put your faith in a mere mortal you can see or the all-powerful God who is invisible. Which will you choose?

> *"Choose for yourselves today the one you will*
> *worship. . . . As for me. . .we will worship Yahweh."*
> JOSHUA 24:15 HCSB

I choose to trust in and serve You, Lord!

* https://biblehub.com/commentaries/judges/21-25.htm.

Torn with Grief

The mother reigns in pride and scorn,
And Hannah's soul with grief is torn.

Elkanah was a good man. A dedicated follower of God. Yet even he had his faults, his doubts, a human penchant for thinking he had an idea that was better than God's. Why else would he bring another woman into his home, one he shared with a wife he loved very much? Did he think his shift to polygamy would be the exception to the general rule that two (or more) women do not a good marriage make?

And who was this second wife? Her name was Peninnah. And too soon Hannah found this other woman bearing her husband his first child, then his second, then his third. Each new birth was a claw tearing at the fabric of whatever self-esteem Hannah may have had left. Peninnah's ability to bear children for Elkanah broke Hannah's heart, consumed her soul with grief, prompting her to mourn for what she once had—a happy marriage with her husband. And for what she may never have: her own child.

One can only imagine all the emotions coursing through her. Rejected, Hannah must have felt demoralized and defective. Her image of herself, her dream of the life she thought she was going to have with her one true love, had been destroyed.

Chances are, those who have struggled with getting or remaining pregnant have wrestled with similar emotions and beliefs. We wonder why having children comes so easily to other women—our friend, sister, or neighbor—yet is such a challenge to us. And we begin to believe we are worth less.

That's when we need to stop listening to the inner voices clamoring to bring us down and see ourselves through God's eyes. Ephesians 2:10 (AMP) tells us:

> For we are His workmanship [His own master
> work, a work of art], created in Christ Jesus
> [reborn from above—spiritually transformed,
> renewed, ready to be used] for good works, which
> God prepared [for us] beforehand [taking paths
> which He set], so that we would walk in them
> [living the good life which He prearranged and
> made ready for us].

Have you ever considered yourself a work of art when you've been forced into early retirement? Has it occurred to you that God has prepared a path that only you can walk, a job only you can do, when you've lost an election? Does it seem as if you're living the good life when the man you thought was Mr. Right breaks your heart and engagement?

When your soul is torn with grief, remember who you are in God's eyes. Then pick yourself up, shake off the dust and remorse, and walk on with your head held high, reminding yourself:

> The LORD will fulfill His purpose for me.
> PSALM 138:8 HCSB

Help me, Lord, to keep my ears, eyes, and heart attentive to You and Your purpose for me. In Jesus' name I pray. Amen.

Choosing Joy

The good man's house, his peaceful tent,
No more is filled with calm content.

*a*ny calm contentment Hannah had once found in her life had flown. For "Peninnah had children, but Hannah was childless" (1 Samuel 1:2 HCSB).

This new arrangement, this two-woman household, had not been brought about by the random action of some stranger. Hannah's own loving husband had opened this door, had allowed this woman who would become Hannah's rival to enter his happy abode. And this was Hannah's new life, one she would need all the grace she could muster to endure. She alone would have to find a way beyond the cries of newborn babes, above the noise that a bevy of growing children can produce, and through the deep despair looming before her.

Perhaps you've been there. Someone you love has brought something into your life and now your contentment has flown. Every routine you once enjoyed is disrupted by this added element.

Consider Habakkuk. He was a prophet living in the final days before the nation of Judah was conquered by the Babylonians. He couldn't understand why God was allowing this to happen. Knowing the enemy would soon be at his country's door, Habakkuk cried out to God for a reprieve. He even gave Him suggestions as to what He (God) should do!

Habakkuk must have felt like Hannah—hopeless, defenseless, and powerless. But he managed to find his hope in God. He remembered who God was: the Holy One whose "splendor and majesty covers the heavens" (Habakkuk 3:3 AMP), whose "brightness is like the sunlight" (verse 4 AMP). God is the One who split the earth, bringing rivers of water to dry land; the One whom mountains saw and trembled; the One who could make the sun and moon stand still; the One who had rescued His people—and could do so again.

With that in mind, Habakkuk found more than contentment. He *chose* joy, writing: "Though the fig tree does not blossom and there is no fruit on the vines, though the yield of the olive fails and the fields produce no food, though the flock is cut off from the fold and there are no cattle in the stalls, yet I will *[choose to]* rejoice in the LORD" (3:17–18 AMP, emphasis added).

Although it may take some effort to rein in your thoughts, to get it together when all around you seems to be falling apart, you too have a choice, however difficult. You too can choose joy, reminding yourself:

The Lord GOD is my strength [my source of courage, my invincible army]; He. . .makes me walk [forward with spiritual confidence] on my high places [of challenge and responsibility].
HABAKKUK 3:19 AMP

Lord, no matter what may be happening in my life,
help me find a way to choose joy in You.

The Pain of Infidelity

But day by day unholy strife
Mars all the joys of wedded life.

Hannah longed for the days when Elkanah had shared no other bed but hers. When his kisses, his embraces were for her alone. Now her bed was often cold. She found it difficult to fall asleep, so accustomed was she to breathing in sync with him. Some evenings when she reached out in the wee hours of the night, she felt only the empty air, his form no longer beside her. It was then she would envision him in the bed of another, the one whose smile of self-satisfaction Hannah would encounter the next day.

Imagine being married to a man you love and who loves you. Now imagine "the other woman"—who in some way does things so much better than you ever could—moving into the bedroom next to yours. Then you'll have some idea of what Hannah was going through.

King Solomon, the man who wrote Proverbs (1:1), had something to say about the keys to a happy marriage. He told men to "drink water from your own well—share your love only with your wife. . . . Let your wife be a fountain of blessing for you. Rejoice in the wife of your youth. She is a loving deer, a graceful doe. Let her breasts satisfy you always. May you always be captivated by her love" (Proverbs 5:15, 18–19 NLT). This is interesting advice considering it comes from Solomon, a man who himself had "700 wives of royal birth and 300 concubines" (1 Kings 11:3 NLT).

Yet the point is well made. There is something so special and holy about the union of one man with one woman. And to have someone else step into the role that was once solely yours is sure to mar whatever marital joy you once shared with that person.

Unfortunately, what looks like infidelity to us was legal polygamy in Hannah's culture. And she had no recourse, legal or otherwise. She had to endure in this "unholy strife."

We can see how such an arrangement would cause Hannah to reimagine not just her present life but her future life with Elkanah. And how no amount of love on his part could repair what he had damaged. In effect, the man had torn asunder their holy union. And Hannah couldn't even go to the local priest or wise man and complain about it!

Today women have more power legally in situations of infidelity. Yet that may not make it any easier for them to bear up under the transgressions of their spouse. Only God can heal and comfort the partners in a marriage that He had intended for two.

He heals the brokenhearted and binds up their wounds
[healing their pain and comforting their sorrow].
PSALM 147:3 AMP

Thank You, Lord, for Your healing touch.

Lord of Hosts

In Shiloh stands Jehovah's court.
Thither the holy tribes resort,
To hold their rites, with one accord,
And feast in peace before the Lord.

The ark of the covenant was in *Shiloh*, a word meaning "rest," an appropriate place for the tent of the tabernacle of the once-wandering Israelites to lie. It had been pitched there by Joshua when "the land was subdued before them" (Joshua 18:1 AMP). And it was from that place, the center of the Promised Land, that he divvied up the land.

It was to Jehovah's court, the holy tabernacle in Shiloh, that all the people of God traveled at least once a year to celebrate the Feast of Unleavened Bread, the Passover, which marked the beginning of the Israelites' journey out of Egypt.

Shiloh was in the territory of Ephraim, the tribe that Joshua belonged to, and thus near his home. That made it convenient for him when he needed to consult with God. The tabernacle remained there throughout most of the days of the judges, a time of about 350 years.

First Samuel 1:3 says it was to Shiloh that Elkanah would come "to worship and to sacrifice to *the LORD of hosts*" (ESV, emphasis added)—the first time that phrase is used in the Bible. It appears in the books of Samuel several more times, and for a total of 260 times in the Old Testament and once in the New Testament (James 5:4).

What does *Yahweh Tseboath*, or "Lord of Hosts," mean? And why does it first appear here, in the beginning of the first book of Samuel?

The phrase "Lord of Hosts" stresses the idea that God rules over all powers—including humans, nature, angels, stars, and other earthly and celestial bodies and beings—in both the material and spiritual realms. He is the all-powerful, almighty entity whom all of creation serves. The title reminds each of us that everything—men, women, and children, forests, brooks, and mountains, suns, moons, and stars, cherubim, seraphim, and archangels—not only worships Him but can be called into service by Him at any time and for any reason.

As to why "Lord of Hosts" appears in 1 Samuel 1 for the first time is anyone's guess. Perhaps the writer wanted to remind God's unruly people that Yahweh Tseboath—not priests nor people—is truly the Lord over all things. That He alone is to be served. That He alone can hear and respond to prayer. That He alone brought His people out of Egypt and into the Promised Land. That He alone is to be worshipped and sacrificed to. Knowing He is Lord over all brings a matchless sense of overwhelming peace.

> *"Be still and know (recognize, understand) that*
> *I am God." . . . The LORD of hosts is with us.*
> PSALM 46:10–11 AMP

> *I let go and give all my concerns to You,*
> *the all-powerful Yahweh Tseboath!*

The Best Plan

Robed in his sacerdotal dress,
Eli the priest is there to bless.

𝒶 t the tabernacle in Shiloh were "the two sons of Eli. . .priests of the Lord" (1 Samuel 1:3 ESV). Eli, the high priest, was old and frail. Because he was unable to serve the Lord as he once had, his sons, also priests, ministered in his place. Still, Eli might well have appeared in his high priestly garb, there to bless people but not do much more.

Yet Eli wasn't only a high priest. He was also a judge of Israel.

In the book of Judges, the people had been doing whatever they wanted, whatever seemed right in their own eyes. This led to a time of anarchy among God's people. But then, when a heroic man or woman would come forward, he or she would gain the favor and the hearts of the people, who would then eagerly serve him or her. But as soon as a judge died, God's people would revert to their old ways, doing whatever they pleased, worshipping whatever god they chose.

The last judge in the book of Judges was Samson. He was followed by Eli, whom we meet in 1 Samuel 1:3. "The country under [Eli]," the *Pulpit Commentary* says, "is prosperous; the Philistines, no longer dominant as in Samson's time, have so felt his power that when they gain a victory the Israelites are astonished at it. Moreover, he is not only judge, he is also high priest."*

As far as career callings go, Eli excelled. But when it came to managing his family, things went sour. For his sons were men who tainted God's priesthood with corruption.

Where did Eli go wrong? After all, the people of Israel loved and respected him. A courageous leader, fighter, and high priest, Eli loved serving God and His people. Yet he could not find it in himself to properly discipline his sons.

When he'd found out all the evil things they'd been doing, no reprimand came from his lips. Only the question "Why are you doing these things?" (1 Samuel 2:23 HCSB), then a second question containing a warning: "If a man sins against another man, God can intercede for him, but if a man sins against the LORD, who can intercede for him?" (verse 25 HCSB). But his sons refused to listen to their loving father. No matter. God had another plan, one that would pave the way for Samuel to become the next high priest.

There's no way to force people, even our own offspring, to do the right thing—or stop doing the wrong thing. All we can do is our best and leave the rest up to God, knowing He has the best plan of all for each one of us.

> *The LORD's plans stand firm forever;*
> *his intentions can never be shaken.*
> PSALM 33:11 NLT

I find peace in knowing, Lord, that no matter
what happens, You have a good plan for all.

* https://biblehub.com/commentaries/1_samuel/1-3.htm.

Honor

Hophni and Phinehas there reside,
And over holy things preside;
Sons of Belial, who disgrace
Their calling and the sacred place.

li's sons were named Hophni and Phinehas. Because of their father and high priest's age and feebleness, they, the unholy duo, ministered in their father's stead over the holy things of God.

In the poet's verses and the King James Bible, they are called "Sons of Belial" (1 Samuel 2:12). *Belial* is a Hebrew word that means "without value" or "worthless." Other versions call them "scoundrels" (NLT) and "wicked" (HCSB).

Their reputations had suffered horribly because they disrespected not only the Lord but their duties as priests. Hophni and Phinehas were creating their own procedures when it came to accepting sacrifices from the people, often sending their servant to demand some of the sacrificial meat be taken out of the pot before it was fully boiled or obtaining it raw so that it could be roasted for them. If anyone protested giving the priests' servant the meat, he would say, "Hand it over right now. If you don't, I'll take it by force!" (1 Samuel 2:16 HCSB).

Eli's sons' contempt for the Lord's offering was very serious in God's eyes. But that wasn't the full extent of their misdeeds. For Eli also heard his sons were "seducing the young women who assisted at the entrance of the Tabernacle" (1 Samuel 2:22 NLT). Yet nothing Eli said would deter them from their behavior. Perhaps that's because "the LORD was already planning to put them to death" (1 Samuel

2:25 NLT). Not only that, but God told Eli, "No one in your family will ever again reach old age. Any man from your family I do not cut off from My altar will bring grief and sadness to you. All your descendants will die violently" (1 Samuel 2:32–33 HCSB). The first proof of God's resolve occurred when both Hophni and Phinehas died on the same day during a battle with the Philistines (1 Samuel 4:10–11).

And who did God blame for the behavior of Hophni and Phinehas? Eli, because he honored his sons more than he did the Lord (1 Samuel 2:29).

God has made it clear that anything we honor more or treat better than we do Him will be removed from us. What are you giving more time, money, or energy to more than God? What do you hold most dear? Who or what do you worship and adore more than Him?

Today, ponder these questions. Take a mental or written inventory of all you love and cherish. Consider where God falls on that list. Then ask Him to help you make whatever adjustments are necessary to keep Him number one in all aspects of your life.

" 'You must love the LORD your God with all your heart, all your soul, and all your mind.' This is the first and greatest commandment."
MATTHEW 22:37–38 NLT

Help me, Lord, to love and worship You above all other people and things. Amen.

Adherence

In Shiloh's court, from year to year,
Elkanah and his house appear.

*E*very year, Elkanah took his family to Shiloh to worship the Lord. And he embarked upon this annual journey despite the fact that unholy priests presided over the holy site and the processing of the sacrifices offered there.

Elkanah's faithfulness in making the yearly trek to Shiloh speaks of his sincere devotion to God. He attended this place of worship year after year, continuing to obey the law of God requiring him, a male Israelite, to present himself before the Lord, in spite of the tabernacle's evil overseers. Elkanah is a wonderful example for all in his adherence to his God and his place of worship—no matter the state of its human leaders.

Today people too easily turn away from their church for various reasons. Perhaps they don't like the old hymns and want to hear more contemporary music. So they go to another church. But once there, they may find the attenders put too much—or not enough—emphasis on prayer. So they decide to visit another church. But there they find the pastor's sermons aren't to their liking or the youth group isn't big enough or the children's programs are poorly run. The list of downsides or upsides of a particular church, its attenders, its programs, its teachers, and its preacher can reach to infinity.

Granted, it can be hard to continue attending a church when some sort of corruption is going on behind the scenes or right in front of you. But once a woman finds a church in which God's truth is spoken and its people abide in Christ and work to study God's Word,

He would have her find a way to help that church. To ascertain her gift and use it to benefit that group of believers. To help "in the work of ministry, to build up the body of Christ, until we all reach unity in the faith and in the knowledge of God's Son" (Ephesians 4:12–13 HCSB). For only when we commit ourselves to a church, its programs and growth, only then will we "no longer be immature like children. We won't be tossed and blown about by every wind of new teaching. We will not be influenced when people try to trick us with lies so clever they sound like the truth" (Ephesians 4:14 NLT).

We each have a special part to play, a unique gift to contribute to help build up the church. What's your gift? In what ways can you rise up out of the pew and become part of the living body? What will you eagerly offer up to your group of fellow believers?

For if the eagerness is there, it is acceptable according to
what one has, not according to what he does not have.
2 CORINTHIANS 8:12 HCSB

Lord, I pray You would tell me what gift
I can offer to Your body of believers.

Family Worship

To worship God, with one accord,
And feast in peace before the Lord.

ach year, Elkanah took his wives and children to Shiloh to worship the Lord and celebrate the Passover together. This custom was something not just encouraged among God's people but
required. For only by including the entire family in the celebration
would the children learn who God was and why He should be worshipped and served.

In preparation for the first Passover, God had told Moses and
Aaron, "Every man shall take for himself a lamb, according to the
house of his father, a lamb for a *household*" (Exodus 12:3 NKJV,
emphasis added). So Moses told the elders, "Pick out and take
lambs for yourselves according to your families, and kill the Passover lamb" (verse 21 NKJV). They were to take the blood of that
lamb and use it to mark the lintel and doorposts of their respective
homes. The people were instructed to then stay inside their homes
that night. And when the Lord came through, He would "not allow
the destroyer to come into your houses to strike" (verse 23 NKJV) the
firstborn within it.

The people were to observe this ordinance for them and their
sons forever. Why? So that when the children would ask why they
were doing this, the parents would have the opportunity to explain
what God had done to save His people from not just death but slav-
ery in Egypt (verses 26–27).

We too can teach our children who God is and what He has
done for us by participating in a meal with our own family of God on

Holy Thursday or Maundy Thursday, a time when we commemorate the Last Supper that Jesus—*our* Passover Lamb—shared with His disciples. We can also humble ourselves, just as Jesus did, by washing feet. For after He had done so, Jesus told them, "I have given you an example to follow. Do as I have done to you. I tell you the truth, slaves are not greater than their master. Nor is the messenger more important than the one who sends the message. Now that you know these things, God will bless you for doing them" (John 13:15–17 NLT).

Just as Jesus taught His followers how to be humble, you can teach your children how to put others before themselves, a lesson especially important in a world where people are increasingly more concerned about themselves than anyone else. And remember, if you yourself don't have children, you can still attend such services and be a humble example for all God's children—no matter what their age.

"I will be the God of all the families of Israel,
and they will be My people."
JEREMIAH 31:1 HCSB

Help me, Father, to be an example to all Your
children. In Jesus' name I pray, amen.

Your Forever Portion

And when from time to time they meet,
And worship at the mercy seat,
Peninnah and her children share
The tokens of the husband's care.

I lkanah brought his entire family—Peninnah and her children, as well as Hannah—to the Passover celebration. There he brought his peace offering to the priest. Putting his hand on the head of the animal, he signaled "that with this gift, which served to nourish and strengthen his own life, he gave up the substance of his life to the Lord, that he might thereby be strengthened both body and soul for a holy walk and conversation," says the *Keil and Delitzsch Bible Commentary on the Old Testament.**

Elkanah then killed his animal offering and watched as its blood was sprinkled against the altar by the priest's own hand and its fat was burned on the altar. This part of the ritual took place, say the commentators, so that "his soul and his inner man might be grounded afresh in the gracious fellowship of the Lord." Finally, Elkanah gave the priest the breast and right leg of the animal. These he waved before the Lord.

The rest of the offering Elkanah prepared for himself and his family. It was a holy meal of love and joy, an example of the spiritual food the Lord uses to sate and renew His people.

From this special sacrifice, this peace offering, this sanctified food, Elkanah "always gave portions of the meat to his wife Peninnah and to each of her sons and daughters" (1 Samuel 1:4 HCSB). In so doing, he proved to be a good and able provider. One can almost envision

Elkanah in a Norman Rockwell type of scene. There he stands at the head of the family table, sharpening his utensils amid the steam rising from his peace offering. He beams with joy, a father and husband proud of his continually growing family, and amazingly blind to the discontent of his first wife, Hannah. Perhaps he laughs at a comment made by his eldest son or looks with fondness upon Peninnah as she helps one young child to eat while breastfeeding another.

All this is witnessed by Hannah, the woman who has no babe at her breast. Yet in this moment, during this celebration, her husband is oblivious to all but the joy and love that surround him.

We've all been there. At a family function, a celebration, perhaps even a holy meal during Easter or Christmas. We try to put on a brave face, hoping others will be oblivious to the emotions we cannot seem to rise above.

Those are the times we need to turn to God. To feed on His offering of peace and to give Him the pain we cannot handle.

My flesh and my heart may fail, but God is the
strength of my heart, my portion forever.
PSALM 73:26 HCSB

Lord, in those times when I cannot rise above
my sorrow, be my forever strength.

* https://biblehub.com/commentaries/1_samuel/1-3.htm.

An Open Heart

*While Hannah's worthier portions prove
The pledges of a dearer love.*

*P*erhaps Elkanah did see the sadness in Hannah's eyes. Perhaps he did have some inkling that his first wife was in some way discontented. Perhaps to cheer her, Elkanah "gave a double portion [of the peace offering] to Hannah" (1 Samuel 1:5 HCSB). He showed favor to Hannah even though "the LORD had shut up her womb" (1:5 KJV).

While Hannah had a house, she didn't exactly have a home. She didn't have any children, the desire of every Jewish woman. Yes, she had a husband who loved her more than wife number two, but she had no sons or daughters. In *All the Women of the Bible*, Herbert Lockyer writes, "Although the Lord had 'shut up her womb' her heart was still open to Him."*

How many of us can say the same? How many of us who yearn for a dream to be fulfilled have turned bitter toward God or lost some part of our faith because He has not yet answered our prayers the way we want Him to? How many of us are so fixated on our desires remaining unfulfilled that we fail to recognize or acknowledge the love others show us? Even worse, what if that love is coming from God and we refuse to open our hearts to it?

There may be times in our lives when, because our fondest dreams go unrealized, we almost lose our footing, almost slip away from God. For, seeing unbelievers' dreams fulfilled, we begin to envy them. We begin to say to ourselves, "They don't have troubles like other people; they're not plagued with problems like everyone else. . . . These fat cats have everything their hearts could ever wish for!" (Psalm 73:5, 7 NLT). Meanwhile, "I get nothing but trouble all day long; every morning brings me pain" (verse 14 NLT).

In times like these we need to understand that the ungodly are the ones headed for trouble—if not in this life, then the one to come. We might realize how bitter our hearts have become and how foolish we must look to God (Psalm 73:21–22 NLT). Hopefully, at that point, we will slip our hand back into His, remembering He is the One we belong to. Each woman can say to herself, "My health may fail, and my spirit may grow weak, but God remains the strength of my heart; he is mine forever" (verse 26 NLT). For then our hearts will open up again—to the God who is love. Although we still long for our dreams to be fulfilled, our hearts won't be bitter because we'll find that we desire God and a relationship with Him more than anything else.

I desire you more than anything on earth.
PSALM 73:25 NLT

May my heart always be open to You,
my Lord, God, Savior, and King. Amen.

* Herbert Lockyer, *All the Women of the Bible* (Grand Rapids: Zondervan, 1967), 65.

Showing Favor

Yearly Elkanah thus bestows
His gifts, and partial favor shows.

*E*ven though Hannah could not produce children for him, Elkanah still loved her best, favoring her above everyone else.

We too are sometimes inclined to have favorites. We may have a friend who is such a kindred spirit that she's able to complete our sentences. Or there may be a child in our life—whether our own or a niece or nephew—to whom we are naturally drawn and can understand more than the others. Both friend and child seem so in tune with us that we can't help but spend more time with them and give more attention to them than all our other friends and family members.

Yet God's Word cautions us against playing favorites. The apostle James comes right out and says, "Do not show favoritism as you hold on to the faith in our glorious Lord Jesus Christ. . . . Indeed, if you keep the royal law prescribed in the Scripture, Love your neighbor as yourself, you are doing well. But if you show favoritism, you commit sin and are convicted by the law as transgressors" (James 2:1, 8–9 HCSB). The apostle Paul, in his letter to young Timothy, gave him explicit advice about how to treat widows, elders, and slaves. And then Paul told him, "I solemnly command you in the presence of God and Christ Jesus and the highest angels to obey these instructions without taking sides or showing favoritism to anyone" (1 Timothy 5:21 NLT).

Why all these warnings about favoritism? Because God showed none. No matter who the person, whether "Jew or Gentile, slave or free, male and female. For you are all one in Christ Jesus" (Galatians 3:28 NLT). And in Acts 10:34–35 (HCSB), Luke records Peter as saying, "Now I really understand that God doesn't show favoritism, but in every nation the person who fears Him and does righteousness is acceptable to Him."

To be imitators of God (Ephesians 5:1), to not just listen to but obey the Word (James 1:22), and to live in harmony with each other (Romans 12:16), we must find a way to treat everyone equally, just as God does (Romans 2:11).

If you're still not convinced, read Genesis 37 and see what happened when Jacob favored Joseph above all his other sons: "When his brothers saw that their father loved him more than all his brothers, they hated him and could not speak peacefully to him" (verse 4 ESV). Then think about how you would feel if someone you loved favored another above you.

"Treat others the same way you want them to treat you."
LUKE 6:31 AMP

Lord, help me to be like You, treating every
person the same. In Your name, amen.

Collateral Damage

And yearly did Peninnah's strife
Mar all the joys of Hannah's life.

Elkanah was a good man. He was dedicated to God, taking his family each year to make a sacrifice to Him. Yet because he chose to follow what was acceptable to the Israelites—but not to God—and have two wives, he experienced trouble in his household.

Hannah, his first wife, the childless one, the one he loved most and favored, was abused by his second wife, Peninnah. "Hannah's rival provoked her bitterly, to irritate and embarrass her, because the LORD had left her childless" (1 Samuel 1:6 AMP).

Ellicott's Commentary for English Readers tells us, "Jealousy, grief, anger, malice, the many bitter fruits of this way of living, so different to God's original appointment, here show themselves. The one sin of polygamy poisons the whole home life of the family, in all other respects apparently a quiet, Godfearing, orderly household."*

It's amazing how one sin can grow to contaminate every single aspect of your life. And it wasn't even Hannah's sin. It was her husband who had taken that step toward polygamy and in so doing "missed the mark." Hannah's mistreatment at Peninnah's hands was just collateral damage.

Polygamy was not against man's law. It was a custom several Old Testament patriarchs picked up from the nations around them. But it did go against God's initial intentions for His people (Genesis 2:22–24). And anything against God's intentions or plans usually brings trouble.

Even today, there are many things not explicitly covered in

the Bible that are lawful in this world but against God's intentions, counter to what God has in mind for His righteous people.

It's not illegal for a man and woman to live together before marriage. But God wants His children to remain chaste until they wed and to be true to each other forever after. Yet in today's society, living together before marriage is more commonplace than ever! Many unwed couples even have a child or multiple children together.

God also commands His people, once married, not to commit adultery. Yet it happens repeatedly and leaves much collateral damage in its wake. Not just for the spouse who is hurt by the infidelity, but also for the children. The picture they've built up in their minds of their mom or dad is suddenly tainted and tattered. How can they ever believe anything that parent tells them from here on out?

Take this opportunity to look at your own life. Consider what you may be doing that is permissible in society but against what God would have you do. Think about whose joy may be marred by your actions. Then ask God to help you change your ways.

You say, "I am allowed to do anything"—
but not everything is good for you.
1 CORINTHIANS 6:12 NLT

Lord, help me see my life through Your eyes
and banish whatever is not good.

* https://biblehub.com/commentaries/1_samuel/1-6.htm.

Peace Plan

Th' accustomed sacrifice is made.
Peace offerings on the board are laid.

$\mathcal{S}$ ome Bible scholars think Hannah (wife number one) and Peninnah (wife number two) were kept in two separate apartments or houses in Ramathaim. Living two separate lives in their home city might have made things a bit more bearable. But their annual road trip to Shiloh must have brought them too close for comfort. For the Bible tells us that Peninnah provoked the barren Hannah "year after year, whenever she went up to the house of the Lord" (1 Samuel 1:7 AMP).

We can only imagine how much Elkanah's favoring Hannah in Shiloh must have fueled Peninnah's ire. Seeing the amount of love and respect he held for wife number one surely stoked the fires within wife number two. Peninnah must have wondered, *How can this man so adore the woman who has given him nothing—when I, Peninnah, have given him child after child? When will enough be enough?!*

How difficult it must have been for Peninnah, Hannah, and Elkanah to worship the Lord under such trying circumstances. For the dynamics among the threesome made for a vicious circle. In Shiloh, Elkanah showed his favor of Hannah, who couldn't bear children. This display brought out the spite and malice Peninnah then inflicted upon Hannah. In turn, Hannah's extreme sorrow prompted Elkanah to show her even more affection, which was then witnessed by Peninnah, and so on, and so on. We might well wonder which of them, if any, could worship the Lord with any kind of calm during this feast of peace.

How about you? What do you need to lay down before the Lord

before a time of prayer and worship? What do you do to settle your heart and mind so that you are focused on God rather than your troubles, your sorrows, or the stress of what is going on around you?

Proverbs 12:20 (ESV) tells us, "Deceit is in the heart of those who devise evil, but those who plan peace have joy." In other words, we must *plan* our peace. We must intentionally pursue, promote, and expect peace by showing kindness to others, giving words of wisdom when asked, and seeking good in all. We must strive to live in peace with others and with ourselves before we go to God to worship. Only then will we be ready vessels into which He may pour His vast supply of peace, strength, hope, and light. For if we wait until we get to church or some other sacred space to cultivate our calm, we will be too filled with turmoil to accept God's provisions for us, forfeiting not just His offering but precious one-to-one moments with the Lord.

Finally, brothers, rejoice. Aim for restoration, comfort
one another, agree with one another, live in peace;
and the God of love and peace will be with you.
2 CORINTHIANS 13:11 ESV

Lord, help me to live in peace so that
Your peace will live in me. Amen.

God's Compassion

The feast is blessed, but peace has flown,
And Hannah grieves and weeps alone.

The priest has blessed the sacrifice Elkanah has brought to the Lord. But there is no peace for the family. For Peninnah has taunted Hannah for her childlessness, making "fun of her because the LORD had kept her from having children. Year after year it was the same— Peninnah would taunt Hannah as they went to the Tabernacle. Each time, Hannah would be reduced to tears" (1 Samuel 1:6–7 NLT).

Most of us have been there. We've taken all we can from those who see our infirmities, weaknesses, or sore spots as bull's-eyes. All their insults, taunts, and barbs have hit their target, leaving us no recourse but to break down in tears. To weep alone.

It happened to Hagar. After she and her son Ishmael, begotten by Abraham, were driven away by Sarah, they wandered aimlessly in the wilderness. When they ran out of water, Hagar put Ishmael in the shade of a bush while she sat down opposite him, several yards away. Unable to watch her son die, she began to weep.

Lost and alone with her tears in the wilderness, Hagar saw no way out of her plight. Yet that's when God made His appearance. He told Hagar He would make her son a great nation. "Then God opened her eyes, and she saw a well of water. So she went and filled the waterskin and gave the boy a drink. God was with the boy, and he grew; he settled in the wilderness" (Genesis 21:19–20 HCSB). And God kept His promise, growing Ishmael into a great nation.

When we cannot find a way out of our misery, when we find ourselves grieving and weeping alone, when we are too raw and shattered to notice or care who sees us weep, when we are lost in the wilderness and cannot take one more step, when we come to the end of our hope, God meets us there.

In our most vulnerable moments, God is there to bring us sustenance, to nourish us, to weep with us. When our hearts are breaking, His is as well. When we are grieving, He grieves with us. Remember Martha? When Jesus saw her crying, in His compassion, He wept too (John 11:33–35).

And when Jesus saw a woman's dead son being carried out of Nain and realized she was a widow, He felt compassion for her. Telling her not to weep, He then raised her son back to life and "gave him back to his mother" (Luke 7:15 NLT).

You never weep alone. Before one tear hits the floor, Jesus comes alongside you, offering you His love, His compassion, and His shoulder. Take it. Take it all.

> *When the Lord saw her, He had compassion*
> *on her and said, "Don't cry."*
> LUKE 7:13 HCSB

Thank You, Lord, for mingling Your love with my tears. Amen.

Quietness and Peace

Fainting beneath the cruel rod,
She cannot eat the feast of God.

The cruel barbs Peninnah inflicted upon Hannah, the taunts about her childlessness, struck her so forcibly that she lost her appetite (1 Samuel 1:7). Such was her anxiety, so great was her pain, so plentiful her tears, that Hannah could not touch one morsel of food at the feast of peace.

The thoughts in our mind can overload our nervous system and shut down or badly impair our digestive process. The writer of Proverbs agrees that our emotional state greatly affects our ability to stomach food: "Better is a dry morsel [of food served] with quietness and peace than a house full of feasting [served] with strife and contention" (17:1 AMP).

Even one of the psalmists writes, "My heart is sick, withered like grass, and I have lost my appetite" (Psalm 102:4 NLT). He recounts his troubles: "My enemies taunt me day after day. They mock and curse me. I eat ashes for food" (verses 8–9 NLT).

The New Living Translation describes Psalm 102 as "a prayer of one overwhelmed with trouble, pouring out problems before the Lord." "Overwhelmed with trouble" is an apt description of Hannah. She too had enemies who taunted her day after day. Not just the provoking Peninnah but Hannah herself. For the things Peninnah was saying to Hannah, the words she was using, were becoming engrained in Hannah's mind, so that even when Peninnah was out of sight, her words continued to echo in Hannah's thoughts, perhaps even becoming part of her inner dialogue.

So what are we to do when the cruel words of another penetrate our thoughts so deeply that they become part of our inner voice? What do we do when, because of our tumultuous thoughts and emotions, our digestive system shuts down, keeping us from adequately receiving and processing the nourishment we need?

First, we identify what we lack: *quietness*. In Proverbs 17:1—"Better is a dry morsel [of food served] with *quietness* and peace than a house full of feasting [served] with strife and contention" (AMP, emphasis added)—the Hebrew word for "quietness" means to be tranquil, to be at peace, to lie still, to be undisturbed.

Now that we know what we lack, how do we get loose from our anxieties, our worldly troubles and sorrows, our own thoughts so that we can have the quietness, the peace we need to eat, to sleep, to live? We seek the One who holds all we need: the Lord. For only there, at His feet, can we find the calm we crave, the peace we pine for.

> *For the Lord God, the Holy One of Israel has said this,*
> *"In returning [to Me] and rest you shall be saved,*
> *in quietness and confident trust is your strength."*
> ISAIAH 30:15 AMP

Lord, please give me the quietness and peace I seek. Amen.

The Cruel Snare

In tenderness Elkanah spake:
"My soul is bleeding for thy sake."

lkanah was so in sympathy with Hannah that her heartache was his. His very soul was bleeding for her sake. Yet Elkanah also must have realized it was his actions that led to her despair. For he alone was the one who took a second wife. Alexander Whyte writes that Elkanah must have known. . .

> *that the greater the wrong done, and the greater*
> *the sorrow caused, the more all that comes back*
> *on him who did the wrong and caused the sorrow.*
> *But, Elkanah. . .never could undo the wrong he*
> *had done to Hannah and to all his house. He could*
> *only take every opportunity to sweeten a little, if*
> *possible, Hannah's great and bitter sorrow. But*
> *such was the cruel snare that Elkanah lay in, that*
> *every effort he made to lighten a little of his own*
> *and Hannah's load, that effort only locked the teeth*
> *of the snare deeper than before into his soul.* *

For every comfort Elkanah tried to provide to Hannah merely led Peninnah to provoke, insult, and injure Hannah even more (1 Samuel 1:4–7).

Although he was a good, tender, loving, and faithful man of God, Elkanah, faced with childlessness, didn't trust in God to provide. He didn't wait for God to remember Hannah and open her womb. Instead, he had his own idea of how to fix things. And, on his own initiative, he took a second wife. Now not only was his first wife suffering, but he was as well. He was reaping what he had sown.

And if Peninnah was such a misery, one can only imagine what her children were like. With such a vicious mother, how could they grow up to be faithful, loving, peace-promoting children of God? Thus, Elkanah's one ungodly choice had led to a multitude of trouble.

Yet don't we at times fall into the same snare? We have a situation that needs to be remedied. We maybe take it to God. Then, before we know it, we've picked it up again and are fretting over it, wondering how to solve our conundrum. Finally, we come up with what we think is a brilliant idea. *Why bother God anymore? I've got the perfect solution.*

We put our scheme in place, telling ourselves, *This is a foolproof plan! I don't see how anything can go wrong!* And then, inevitably, it does.

And this scenario doesn't happen just once, but over and over again!

The remedy? Engraving the following words from Proverbs upon our minds and hearts. In doing so, we may just avoid the next cruel snare.

> *Trust in the LORD with all your heart, and do not lean on your own understanding. In all your ways acknowledge him, and he will make straight your paths.*
> PROVERBS 3:5–6 ESV

Lord, may You be the only Master Planner in my life. Amen.

* Alexander Whyte, "Hannah," in *Alexander Whyte's Dictionary of Bible Characters* (1901), www.studylight.org/dictionaries/eng/wbc/h/hannah.html.

Burden Bearing

"The pangs that wound thy heart I share,
And all thy anguish I could bear."

Whatever Hannah suffered, Elkanah felt in his own heart. That's how great his love was for her (1 Samuel 1:5). When he saw her so discontent, weeping, unable to eat, he wanted to bear her anguish, to take her grief upon himself.

Perhaps you have felt the same way. When someone you love suffers pain, you feel it within yourself. Because your hearts and spirits are so aligned, your wish is to take all her troubles upon yourself. That kind of love, that kind of empathy you have for another is the same kind of love God has for us.

Imagine the degree of love, empathy, and compassion that would move the Creator to send down His only Son to save His people, many of whom not only didn't know but didn't *love* God. And yet the Father sent Him anyway, to live among people who had gone astray.

The Son was born to a humble couple in a humble barn. The child was not overly handsome. In fact, there was nothing about Him to attract us at all. He was not just hated but rejected. A "man of sorrows, acquainted with deepest grief" (Isaiah 53:3 NLT).

This grief Jesus was acquainted with was not just the usual grief derived from sickness and disease but also grief derived from anxiety, affliction, evils, and calamities—and felt in both body and soul. *Ellicott's Commentary for English Readers* says, "In the Gospel, we. . .have evidence of an organisation every nerve of which thrilled with its sensitiveness to pain, and was quickly exhausted.

The intensity of His sympathy made Him feel the pain of others as His own."*

In Luke 8:46, when the woman with the issue of blood touched the hem of Jesus' garment, so sensitive was He that He actually felt His healing power streaming out of Him and into her. In John 4:6, so humanly weary was He from His journeying that He rested by a well, giving Him a chance to chat and change the life of a Samaritan woman. Because of all those Jesus healed and cleansed, "he fulfilled Isaiah's well-known revelation: He took our illnesses, he carried our diseases" (Matthew 8:17 MSG).

Because of God's love for us, He sent His Son, Jesus, to die for us so that we could have eternal life with the Father (John 3:16). And He did this even while we were still not living up to His plans for us (Romans 5:8).

There is no way we can repay what God and Jesus in their love bore for us. But what we can do is be to others as Elkanah was for Hannah.

Bear one another's burdens, and so fulfill the law of Christ.
GALATIANS 6:2 ESV

Help me be a willing and loving burden bearer, Lord.

* https://biblehub.com/commentaries/isaiah/53-3.htm.

Four Questions: Part 1

"Sweet Hannah! Let thy sorrows cease.
Say to thy troubled spirit, Peace.
Why weep? Thy husband's love will prove
Better to thee than children's love."

Every year that the family went to Shiloh, Peninnah would cruelly taunt the childless Hannah. And every year, Hannah would be reduced to tears and lose her appetite. And, apparently, every year Elkanah would ask Hannah four questions: "Why are you crying? . . . Why won't you eat? Why are you troubled? Am I not better to you than 10 sons?" (1 Samuel 1:8 HCSB).

Let's take first things first. A man is asking a woman, "Why are you crying?" This reminds us of another scene, one from the New Testament. For it is there we read of another caring man, the now-resurrected Jesus, asking Mary Magdalene, "Woman, why are you crying? For whom are you looking?" (John 20:15 AMP). It seems both men knew the answers to their questions.

Elkanah must have known why Hannah was crying because he had to have overheard (or heard about) Peninnah's taunts. And unless he was blind and deaf, he had to have known (from experience, if nothing else) that when Hannah was very upset, she found it hard to eat, no matter what was placed before her. And he had to know she was troubled because she was unable to bear him any children. His follow-up question—"Am I not better to you than 10 sons?"—proves it.

And Jesus must have known not only why Mary Magdalene was crying but also whom she was looking for. Because He was not just a man but also God. And God knows everything.

Perhaps Jesus asked Mary why she was crying because there He stood. Why weep when the person you are longing for—and *looking for*—is standing right in front of you, asking you questions?

So why do these two men ask the women why they are crying?

Jesus may have been asking because He wanted Mary to look through her tears and recognize Him, to realize that all was well because He had risen.

Elkanah may have asked Hannah questions because he was a man concerned about his wife. Men are born protectors. And how can a man protect a woman, how can he "fix" his beloved's problems, unless he knows specifically what she is crying about?

Perhaps both Jesus and Elkanah wanted to give the women they addressed some time to calm down. Perhaps they wanted those women to know that they saw their distress, that they were concerned about their troubles, that they were there to listen—no matter how much pain the tears and the reason for them caused both the lover and the beloved. And sometimes, that's all a woman needs.

> *You keep track of all my sorrows. You have*
> *collected all my tears in your bottle.*
> PSALM 56:8–9 NLT

Thank You, Lord, for counting my tears as precious to You. Amen.

Four Questions: Part 2

"Sweet Hannah! Let thy sorrows cease.
Say to thy troubled spirit, Peace.
Why weep? Thy husband's love will prove
Better to thee than children's love."

Elkanah's last of four questions to the weeping Hannah was "Am I not better to you than 10 sons?" (1 Samuel 1:8 HCSB). In other words, aren't the love of a husband and the man himself better than the love and presence of children?

That's a challenging question for any woman to answer. For how can a woman get a man to understand her deep yearning to conceive, birth, and care for a child? Her intense and innate desire to hold a helpless infant in her arms and nourish it with the milk from her breast? To teach the child how to eat, speak, walk, run, play, and love? Let's face it: there are some things in a woman's life that a man's love cannot replace, replicate, or repair.

One might wonder what Elkanah would say if Hannah asked him the same question: "Husband, am I not better to you than 10 sons?" Apparently, she and her love were not enough, or else Elkanah would not have taken a second wife.

Yet perhaps Elkanah's question had a different meaning. Perhaps he knew the jealous Peninnah would have traded places with Hannah in a heartbeat, forsaking the ability to conceive and bear children for the genuine love, affection, and adoration of her husband.

Sisters Leah and Rachel were in such a predicament. Jacob had fallen in love with the fair Rachel and offered to serve her father, Laban, seven years for her hand in marriage. Laban agreed, but on the wedding night, "when it was dark, Laban took Leah to Jacob, and he slept with her" (Genesis 29:23 NLT). The next morning, in the light of day, Jacob realized he'd been tricked into marrying the older sister, Leah. Laban told him if he waited until the bridal week was over, Jacob would be given Rachel too—in exchange for another seven years of labor.

Jacob agreed. And although it was the barren Rachel he loved, it was the unloved Leah who gave him four sons before Rachel's womb was opened.

Although we don't know or understand why God closes the wombs of some and opens the wombs of others, we do know, as Genesis frequently points out, that He is the One who ultimately creates human life. And He, as Jeremiah tells us, is the One who has the grand plan for each of us. Our work is to trust Him with all details without worrying why.

Take delight in the LORD, and He will give you your heart's desires. Commit your way to the LORD; trust in Him, and He will act, making your righteousness shine like the dawn, your justice like the noonday.
PSALM 37:4–6 HCSB

I commit all my desires and plans to You, Lord, entrusting them into Your hands. In Jesus' name, amen.

A Word on Words: Part 1

As fall on thirsty land the showers,
Or dew distills on drooping flowers,
So gentle tones of love impart
Revivings to the weary heart.

Elkanah's kind, loving, and soothing words (1 Samuel 1:8) may have had some effect on the weeping and nauseous Hannah (verse 7). For 1 Samuel 1:9 (ESV) tells us, "After they had eaten and drunk in Shiloh, Hannah rose." Thus, she had apparently pulled herself together enough to sit at the feast table and take some nourishment, if only a little.

Words. They can make you or break you. They can build you up or tear you down. They can be used to move mountains or bring floodwaters back together.

God knew the power of words. For that is what He used to bring creation into being, order to chaos, and light to darkness. He said, " 'Let there be light,' and there was light" (Genesis 1:3 NLT).

Perhaps Hannah too knew the power of words. After hearing Peninnah's cruel words intended to wound and maim her heart, mind, body, and soul, Hannah could have said something harsh to Peninnah in reply. Yet the author of Samuel records no instance of Hannah even opening her mouth.

Perhaps she was one who guarded her mouth to preserve her life, instead of opening her lips and coming to ruin (Proverbs 13:3). Perhaps Hannah, knowing that "the words of the reckless pierce like swords, but the tongue of the wise brings healing" (Proverbs 12:18 NIV), was unsure how to respond to Peninnah and so worked to restrain her own words (Proverbs 17:27).

Perhaps Hannah, no matter how much she despaired over her rival's words, was too gentle in heart and of tongue to say something that might break Peninnah's spirit (Proverbs 15:4), as she had broken Hannah's. Perhaps Hannah figured if she said something in haste, she would bring even more trouble upon herself than she already had (Proverbs 21:23).

Oh that we would be more like Hannah and less like Peninnah. That we would work to consider our words and their power before they ever leave our mouths. That we would keep our mouths shut, our words to ourselves when there is no hope of any of them making a situation better.

Yet how do we keep our tongues from speaking evil and our lips from telling lies (Psalm 34:13)? How do we make sure our words are gracious like "a honeycomb, sweet to the soul and healing to the bones" (Proverbs 16:24 NIV)? We look to followers of God who are wiser than ourselves. And we look to the Word of God.

May the words of my mouth and the meditation of my heart
be pleasing to you, O LORD, my rock and my redeemer.
PSALM 19:14 NLT

Lord, may my words and thoughts be pleasing
to You and a blessing to others. Amen.

A Word on Words: Part 2

And thus the Levite's words console
The anguish of the grieved one's soul
And Hannah, and the household meet,
And feast before the mercy seat.

The words of Delilah brought down Samson: "When she pressured him day after day with her words and pleaded with him, he was annoyed to death" (Judges 16:16 AMP). Finally, he told her it was his hair that gave him his strength. And it was that information that Delilah, a paid informant, gave to his enemies so they could cut him down to size.

It was the words of Ruth—"Wherever you go, I will go, and wherever you live, I will live; your people will be my people, and your God will be my God" (Ruth 1:16 HCSB)—that eventually turned Naomi's life from bitterness to bliss.

It was the words and desire of a little servant girl to her mistress—"I wish my master would go to see the prophet in Samaria. He would heal him of his leprosy" (2 Kings 5:3 NLT)—that brought Naaman, an Aramean army commander, not only healing but the knowledge of the God who heals.

And it was the cruel words of Peninnah that tormented and grieved Hannah, and the encouraging words of Elkanah that brought relief to his wife, just "like cold water to a weary soul" (Proverbs 25:25 NIV).

So how can we make sure our words lift up instead of tear down? We can "think carefully before speaking" (Proverbs 15:28 NLT) and look to God's Word for instruction.

Jesus said clearly, "On the day of judgment people will give account for every careless word they speak" (Matthew 12:36 ESV). *That's* something to stop a woman in her tracks. How many words have you spoken that may, in the end, either save you or condemn you? Jesus goes on to remind us, "Words are powerful; take them seriously. Words can be your salvation. Words can also be your damnation" (Matthew 12:37 MSG).

Our words are a testimony, a statement that declares who we are! James writes, "If you claim to be religious but don't control your tongue, you are fooling yourself, and your religion is worthless" (James 1:26 NLT). Ouch! That statement might hurt, but it is the truth. If we can't control our tongue, if we can't help but spew out harsh words that hurt and maim, who would want to follow the God we profess?

Below is a good rule of thumb to follow to keep you on the right side of your mouth:

Watch the way you talk. Let nothing foul or dirty come out
of your mouth. Say only what helps, each word a gift.
EPHESIANS 4:29 MSG

Help me, Lord, to make each word from my
lips a gift to myself and others. Amen.

Seeking God

The sacrifice and feast are o'er,
And Hannah seeks the temple door.

Having received some comfort from Elkanah's words, Hannah takes some nourishment at the "sacrificial meal at Shiloh" in an attempt to please her husband; then, still burdened, still needing relief from her distress, Hannah "got up and went to pray" (1 Samuel 1:9 NLT) in the tabernacle. Having fulfilled her duty, her outward obligation, Hannah sought succor for her inner woes.

In *All the Women of the Bible*, Herbert Lockyer writes, "Childless, Hannah was not prayerless. Barren, she still believed, and her pain found a refuge in prayer."*

How many of us would say the same? How many of us, tired of waiting for an answer to prayer, have just given up—not only on our desires but on our God—and so have stopped seeking Him, stopped praying, stopped making Him an integral part of our lives?

Not so with Hannah. She was a woman who was not to be dissuaded from her intense desire to birth a child. So she followed the counsel of Moses. She searched for the Lord her God, knowing she would find Him when she sought Him with all her heart and soul (Deuteronomy 4:29). For there was no other person, no other power to whom she could appeal.

Hannah had decided to seek God, to inquire of Him and commit her cause to Him, fully believing that He could, would, and did do "great and unsearchable things, marvelous things without number" (Job 5:9 AMP). If her God could divide the seas, move mountains, bring water out of rocks, and make the sun and moon stand still, surely He could make one faithful and good yet barren woman able to bear a child.

Jesus Himself encouraged us to pray and to never give up, telling us:

> *"Ask and keep on asking and it will be given to you; seek and keep on seeking and you will find; knock and keep on knocking and the door will be opened to you. For everyone who keeps on asking receives, and he who keeps on seeking finds, and to him who keeps on knocking, it will be opened." (Matthew 7:7–8 AMP)*

Unlike Hannah, you don't have to go to a tabernacle to pray. You can pray right where you are. For "He is not far from each one of us" (Acts 17:27 AMP). But you must approach Him with the humble attitude hinted at in 1 Chronicles 16:11 (AMP): "Seek the LORD and His strength; seek His face continually [longing to be in His presence]."

Pick up those desires you may have left by the wayside. Present them to God with a seeking spirit and a prayerful attitude, longing to meet Him heart to heart.

> *Seek the LORD while you can find him.*
> *Call on him now while he is near.*
> ISAIAH 55:6 NLT

Lord, my refuge, I come seeking You in prayer. . . .

* Herbert Lockyer, *All the Women of the Bible* (Grand Rapids: Zondervan, 1967), https://www.biblegateway.com/devotionals/all-women-bible/3995/08/14.

Throne of Grace

Near to the throne of grace, and there
She pours her soul to God in prayer. . . .

Before the throne of grace, Hannah lets down her great burden. About this wonderfully vivid scene, Herbert Lockyer writes:

> *While thousands of women prayed before Hannah's*
> *day, hers is the first recorded instance of a woman*
> *at prayer. There are relatively few illustrations*
> *of women praying, because women appear in*
> *the Bible. . .less frequently than men. If only we*
> *had the story of devout women from Eve down to*
> *Hannah, what prayer-watchers we would see them*
> *to be. Certainly the world owes more to the prayers*
> *of women than it realizes.**

President Abraham Lincoln knew the power and value of a woman's petitions to God. For he was quoted as saying, "I remember my mother's prayers and they have followed me. They have clung to me all my life."

What a portrait of prayer we see in this scene. How well the humility of Hannah is demonstrated. How clear the power and potency of the throne of grace she approached so reverently and boldly.

Grace is the help God gives us, the help He desires us to have—and not necessarily because of anything we have done to earn it. It is the unmerited favor He delights to bestow upon us, simply because He loves us!

Hannah couldn't apply to Elkanah to gift her with a baby. They'd been lying together for years with no success. If Hannah was ever going to be blessed with a baby, God was her only recourse, her only resource.

Thankfully Hannah didn't take her cues from Rachel, who, having yet to bear any children to Jacob, became jealous of her sister, Leah, for birthing him many. For a remedy, Rachel demanded of her husband, "Give me sons, or I will die!" (Genesis 30:1 HCSB). Jacob, in response, made it clear to his wife that God alone could deny or allow a woman her children.

Nor did Hannah take Sarah's route, giving a slave woman to her husband to bear children for her. Instead, she applied directly to her gracious God.

Thank God that we who believe in Jesus can draw near that same throne of grace with confidence, knowing "we may receive mercy and find grace to help in time of need" (Hebrews 4:16 ESV). Even better, we have Jesus as our high priest "who understands our weaknesses" (Hebrews 4:15 NLT).

Today, take your heartaches to the throne of grace with confidence, humility, and expectation. Do so with the power and understanding of Jesus behind you and the assurance of Hannah within you.

God is passionate that the spirit he has placed within us should be faithful to him. And he gives grace generously. As the Scriptures say, "God opposes the proud but gives grace to the humble."
JAMES 4:5–6 NLT

Source of joy, love, and grace, please hear my humble prayer.

* Herbert Lockyer, *All the Prayers of the Bible* (Grand Rapids: Zondervan, 1959), 60.

Bathed in Tears

And every thought is bathed in tears
Gathered from woes of many years.

H annah, having swallowed back the tears prompted by the end-less provocations of Peninnah, had managed to eat some of the food from the feast table but not much. And now, as she entered the tabernacle, a deluge of tears flowed from the barren woman once more. For the Bible tells us, "Hannah was greatly distressed, and she prayed to the Lord and wept in anguish" (1 Samuel 1:10 AMP).

Perhaps you've been where Hannah was. So much grief lies within you, so many sorrows you have been shouldering for days, weeks, months, perhaps even years. No longer can you just bite your lip or clench your fists and plaster that fake smile upon your face, doing all you can to stanch the barrage of tears that simmers beneath the surface. The dam has broken and there's no way to stop the water cascading down your cheeks, nor stifle the convulsive sobs.

You might feel that when you're bottling up all your tears inside you're just being brave. You're just employing that stiff upper lip you've been taught to show. Meanwhile, God is wondering where you are, why your tears are not being shed upon His breast. After all, He sent His Son so that you would be able to approach Him and pour out all your woes and worries.

God doesn't want us to store up all our grief within ourselves until we're ready to burst. He wants us to run to Him for comfort whenever anything disturbs the peace and calm He has planted within us. By design, He made our bodies capable of producing tears, the releasing of which relieves our stress, lowers our blood pressure, and removes certain toxins from our bodies.

So cry! Acknowledge the feelings you're trying to suppress and communicate them to others, including the Lord of your life! When you bring Him yourself—not the persona you're trying to convey to others but your true self with all your worries and imperfections—He is moved to move on your behalf. *The Message* puts it this way: "Hit bottom, and cry your eyes out. The fun and games are over. Get serious, really serious. Get down on your knees before the Master; it's the only way you'll get on your feet" (James 4:9–10 MSG).

So go to God with all your burdens. Lay them at His feet. Allow your tears to fall upon His shoulder and ask Him to relieve your distress so that later you may rise and say:

Return to your rest, my soul, for the LORD has been
good to you. For You, LORD, rescued me from death,
my eyes from tears, my feet from stumbling.
PSALM 116:7–8 HCSB

I come to You today, Lord, with a tear
in my eye and a prayer upon my lips.

Hannah's Prayer Begins

"O Lord of hosts! in agony
Thy handmaid lifts her cries to Thee."

annah's wordless prayer begins. And it begins with the aspect of God she is addressing: the "Lord of Hosts" (1 Samuel 1:11 HCSB).

The first time in the Bible this name is applied to God appears in verse 3 of this same chapter: "This man [Elkanah] would go up from his town every year to worship and to sacrifice to the Lord of Hosts at Shiloh" (1:3 HCSB). And now it appears for the second time to signify the One to whom Hannah addresses her silent prayer, the One in whose presence she sheds her tears. To gain the desire of her heart, her wish above all other wishes, she applies to the "great and mighty God, whose name is the Lord of hosts" (Jeremiah 32:18 ESV).

This same Lord of Hosts is the One who spoke through Malachi: "Bring the full tithe into the storehouse, that there may be food in my house. And thereby put me to the test, says the Lord of hosts, if I will not open the windows of heaven for you and pour down for you a blessing until there is no more need" (Malachi 3:10 ESV).

This is the Lord who has an army of angels at His disposal, such as those who appeared in Luke 2:13 (AMP): "Then suddenly there appeared with the angel a multitude of the heavenly host (angelic army) praising God."

This Creator and Lord over all beings, all nature, all worlds was the One Hannah envisioned in her mind as she was praying her heart out for the one thing she desired above all others: a child. And she was praying this prayer in that Lord's house, in the dwelling place of the One who had performed miracle after miracle for His people. For that's what Hannah needed in this moment: a miracle.

Hannah's prayer to the Lord of Hosts may remind us of Psalm 84, which is thought to be a psalm pilgrims sang on their way to the temple in Jerusalem: "Even the sparrow finds a home, and the swallow a nest for herself, where she may lay her young, at your altars, O LORD of hosts, my King and my God" (verse 3 ESV).

Just as our great and mighty Lord of Hosts provides a place within His own dwelling for the lowly sparrow, His ears and eyes are open to the prayers and pleas of the lowliest of His servants. Servants such as Hannah. Servants such as you. Not one of your heartfelt pleas will fall to the ground unheard and unheeded (Matthew 10:29–31).

So take your tears and prayers and petitions, as well as your praises, to the Lord of Hosts. Remember how much He cares for you and longs to fulfill your desires. Begin by praying. . .

LORD God of Hosts, hear my prayer; listen. . .
PSALM 84:8 HCSB

"See Me"

*"My heart is sore, my spirit faints
Beneath the load of my complaints."*

Hannah's silent prayer begins with the words "LORD of Hosts, if You will take notice of Your servant's affliction" (1 Samuel 1:11 HCSB). She asks for God to "see her." To truly take notice of who she is and what she has been going through, how heartsick she has become, how much her spirit is downcast beneath this load of complaints that she has been carrying.

We all want and need to be seen, to be recognized. We need others to understand what we have been and are going through so that they will understand the pain we feel, the suffering we've endured. We want them to be able to fathom the depths of our disappointment and discouragement.

Chances are you've been there. You too have come before God and wanted Him to take notice of what you've been dealing with, how hard your road has been, how much grief you've borne. Whether or not that suffering has come from something you did (intentionally or not) or something that was done to you doesn't matter. In this case, suffering is suffering. The source doesn't really matter.

You'll notice that Hannah's suffering was brought about by two things out of her control. The first was biological: for some reason, she was unable to conceive a child. The second was her husband's second wife who taunted her unmercifully because she was barren. Yet Hannah never laid any blame at either God's feet or Peninnah's. She merely wanted God to *see* her situation and to hear her prayer and answer it.

God doesn't just see suffering. He draws near to those who are suffering and reaches out to save them (Psalm 34:18). When Hagar had conceived a baby by Abraham and then fled from his wife, Sarah, she found herself by a spring in the wilderness. It was there God found her, gave her direction, and comforted her with His promises. Afterward "she called the name of the LORD who spoke to her, 'You are God Who Sees'; for she said, 'Have I not even here [in the wilderness] remained alive after seeing Him [who sees me with understanding and compassion]?' " (Genesis 16:13 AMP).

Jesus too saw the suffering of His people. And because of what He saw, He "felt [profound] compassion for them and healed their sick" (Matthew 14:14 AMP). Then, before He left to be with the Father, He promised to send them a Comforter, an Advocate, a Helper who is merely a prayer away (John 16:7).

Today, know that you have a God who sees you *and* your suffering. That He has compassion and comfort for you, that He understands what you are going through. And that help is just a prayer away.

"For the eyes of the LORD move to and fro throughout the earth
so that He may support those whose heart is completely His."
2 CHRONICLES 16:9 AMP

Lord, please see me.

"Hear Me"

"O Lord! If Thou will hear my voice. . ."

annah, already having asked the Lord of Hosts to see her, to acknowledge her, now asks God to *hear* her, to recognize her voice, to remember who she is and what she has gone through and continues to go through. She wants Him to bend His listening ear down to her humble lips.

When we ask someone to listen to us, we are attempting not just to impart knowledge to them and, in the process, unburden ourselves, but to have them understand us. Then, when we are certain they are listening, we find ourselves trusting them to hold our deepest secrets. Knowing someone is attentive to what we're saying also lifts our self-esteem, making us feel that we and what we have to say are important in our listener's eyes.

That's just how God, the holiest and most powerful of listeners, wants us to feel about Him. He wants us to understand that we can tell Him, who already knows everything, *anything*. He wants us to realize that He will understand what we're saying even if we're not able to put it into words. He wants us to know that He hears us and that what we're telling Him is important. And that we can trust Him with the secrets we reveal when we open and unfold our heart, soul, and spirit to Him.

We know God hears our prayers and listens to our voices, our cries, our groans, distinguishing them from all others. David writes, "In my distress [when I seemed surrounded] I called upon the Lord and cried to my God for help; He heard my voice from His temple, and my cry for help came before Him, *into His very ears*" (Psalm 18:6

AMP, emphasis added). Imagine—you open your mouth and God recognizes your voice just as you recognize His (John 10:27–28). *And* He knows what you're going to say to Him before you have even begun to lift up your words to His waiting ears (Psalm 139:4)!

Why does God hear your prayer? Why does He listen to your voice? Because you are faithful to Him, reverently fear Him, and wholeheartedly worship Him (Psalms 4:3; 145:19; John 9:31). Because you abide by His will, and in so doing, you do right (Psalm 34:15; Proverbs 15:29; 1 Peter 3:12). Because you fully believe in Him (1 John 5:14).

If we don't tick all those boxes, God will still hear our prayers. But the more right we are with Him, the more effective and in line with His will our prayers will be.

The next time you pray, check your heart and soul. Be sure your hands and spirit are clean. Then, after you pray, you'll be able to say. . .

God has listened; He has paid attention to the sound of my prayer.
PSALM 66:19 HCSB

Lord, hear my prayer. . . .

"Answer Me"

"If Thou will. . .bid me know a mother's joys. . ."

annah has already asked God to see her, to "take notice of [His] servant's affliction" (1 Samuel 1:11 HCSB). She has asked God to hear her, recognize her voice, listen to her pour out her sorrows. And now we come to the last of her three requests: that God answer her prayer and grant her a son.

You might say that's a big ask for a barren woman. But Hannah knows how big her God is. After all, she *is* submitting her request to the Lord of Hosts. And He, Creator of all things, has all the power and might to grant, to do, whatever He is requested or desires to do.

Hannah had cried out to her Lord with no malice in her heart toward anyone (Psalm 66:17–20) about the treatment she had been receiving because of her physical condition. She had faith that God understood her and her situation, that He knew her comings and goings, the secrets of her heart (Psalm 121:8; Jeremiah 17:10). She had confidence that "He fulfills the desires of those who fear Him; He hears their cry for help and saves them" (Psalm 145:19 HCSB).

We can have that same confidence. Perhaps even more! Because we had God Himself in the flesh, Jesus our Savior, promise us:

> *"I assure you and most solemnly say to you, if you*
> *have faith [personal trust and confidence in Me]*
> *and do not doubt or allow yourself to be drawn*
> *in two directions, you will not only do what was*
> *done to the fig tree, but even if you say to this*
> *mountain, 'Be taken up and thrown into the sea,'*

it will happen [if God wills it]. And whatever
you ask for in prayer, believing, you will receive."
(Matthew 21:21–22 AMP)

What a promise! That if we don't allow our doubts to tear apart our faith, that if what we ask is within God's will, *we will receive it. That* is confidence. And all it takes is believing that our God is big enough, mighty enough, loving enough to meet our needs, to prove His promises, to grant our requests.

If you have that confidence and you are walking in step with God, your prayers will be powerful (James 5:16) and answered before you even approach Him (Isaiah 65:24).

Do you have a pressing need? Do you have the confidence to approach God with it now? Do you believe He is strong enough and resourceful enough to grant your request no matter how improbable or impossible it seems in your own eyes? If your heart is right, go to God now, believing He is already working to answer your prayer.

If we know that He hears whatever we ask, we know
that we have what we have asked Him for.
1 JOHN 5:15 HCSB

Lord, I pray You would see me. Hear me. Answer my prayer.

Hannah's Vows

"Thy handmaid's son will I resign,
And he shall be forever Thine.
No razor shall his locks displace,
But he shall stand with all his grace
Within Thy courts, before Thy sight,
A consecrated Nazarite."

Hannah has gone before the Lord of Hosts and brought Him her conditions, her "ifs," saying to God, "*If* you will see me, hear me, and answer my prayer for a son. . ." Now she is ready to present her two vows, her "thens": *Then* "I will give him to the LORD all the days of his life, and his hair will never be cut" (1 Samuel 1:11 HCSB, emphasis added). In other words, Hannah not only will give her gift from God (a son) back to Him but will raise him as a Nazirite (Numbers 6).

In Hannah's address to God and her vows within that address, she distinguishes herself in three ways. The first is that from the day of creation, no human had called God the "Lord of Hosts"—until Hannah. And she was a woman. The second is that under Levitical law, a vow made by a woman had to be confirmed by a man. We suspect Hannah's vow would be affirmed by her husband, Elkanah. But she broke another norm. For it was a tradition among the Jews that only a *man* could vow a son to be a Nazirite. And here Hannah is making that vow herself! What courage—prompted by desperation!

One might wonder why this woman, this barren woman, would break the norms, perform these firsts, and plead for a son she would have to give back to God. Perhaps Hannah knew the peril her people were in. Perhaps she knew that both God *and* His people needed a special man, a priest, a leader who would walk closely with God and usher in a new beginning for them all.

To date, the Israelites had only had judges. And even they could not keep the people of God from turning their backs on Him. Even the priesthood was in decay! The two who served at the tabernacle, Eli's sons Hophni and Phinehas, were not only disobeying God's sacrificial laws and bereft of any faith in the Lord but sleeping with the women who served at the tent's entrance (1 Samuel 2:12–17, 22–25)!

Both God and country needed a good leader, one who would be strong, righteous, undefiled. And Hannah, a humble handmaiden, was a pious conduit offering herself up to God for that mission. Her request would meet both her intense desire and God's.

May all the requests you make to God meet His desire as well as yours.

Let God transform you into a new person by changing the way you think. Then you will learn to know God's will for you, which is good and pleasing and perfect.
ROMANS 12:2 NLT

Lord, renew my mind so that my desires align with Yours.

Silent Prayer

'Twas silent prayer. The weeping eye,
The face that spake of agony.

Hannah had presented her vows to God, saying that if God gave her a son, she would give him back to God and never cut his hair. As she did this, she was weeping bitterly (1 Samuel 1:10) and "praying silently, and though her lips were moving, her voice could not be heard" (verse 13 HCSB).

About this scene we learn from Herbert Lockyer's *All the Prayers of the Bible* that not only was Hannah's "the first recorded instance of a woman at prayer" but "the first instance in the Bible of silent or mental prayer. Hers was a groaning that could not be uttered." He writes,

> *Words are not essential to the offering of true prayer, though they often help in the expression of our thoughts and desires. At times, however, the heart is too full for utterance, or the presence of others, as in Hannah's case, make articulate prayer impossible. . . . Prayer is the soul's desire whether it is uttered or unexpressed.**

We've all been there, our hearts so heavy we were driven to prayer but unable to put our thoughts, our sorrows, our fears, our pain, our frustrations into words.

Over five hundred years after Hannah, Nehemiah, an exiled Jew and a cupbearer to King Artaxerxes in Persia, was given the news that the walls of Jerusalem had been broken down and its gates burned. He writes, "When I heard these words, I sat down and wept. I mourned for a number of days, fasting and praying before the God of heaven" (Nehemiah 1:4 HCSB).

Days later, when he presented wine to the king, his grief was so obvious the king asked him what was wrong. Nehemiah said, "Why should I not be sad when the city where my ancestors are buried lies in ruins and its gates have been destroyed by fire?" (2:3 HCSB). When Artaxerxes asked how he could help, Nehemiah sent up a silent prayer to the God of heaven before he replied (2:4).

And God must have answered that prayer. For the king not only allowed Nehemiah to go back to Jerusalem but wrote him letters to governors of the regions he'd be traveling through so that he'd have safe passage and another letter to the "keeper of the king's forest, so that he will give me timber to rebuild" (2:8 HCSB).

When your heart is so wounded and torn that you cannot find the words to pray, pray anyway. For the Holy Spirit will be on hand to do your talking for you.

> *The Spirit helps us in our weakness. For we do not know*
> *what to pray for as we ought, but the Spirit himself*
> *intercedes for us with groanings too deep for words.*
> ROMANS 8:26 ESV

> *Thank You, Lord, for giving us Your Spirit when*
> *our spirits are too heavy for words.*

* Herbert Lockyer, *All the Prayers of the Bible* (Grand Rapids: Zondervan, 1959), 60–61.

Prayer Postures

The moving lips, the bowed down head,
The arms upraised, the hands outspread. . .

Our poet takes some liberties, veering away from scripture to present a visual picture of Hannah as she is praying silently to her Lord of Hosts. As her lips move, her head is bowed, her arms raised, her hands spread out. All speak of a person in fervent but silent prayer to her Lord. She laid out everything before Him, including herself.

That was Hannah's prayer posture. But it doesn't have to be everyone's.

Although the most important aspect of your prayer posture is the position of your heart, soul, and spirit (Psalm 51:17), it's still a good idea to consider various ways you can humble yourself before the Lord.

One is *praying while lying down*: "On your bed, reflect in your heart and be still" (Psalm 4:4 HCSB).

The second and third are *praying on your knees* and *with your arms outstretched*: "As Solomon finished offering all this prayer and plea to the LORD, he arose from before the altar of the LORD, where he had knelt with hands outstretched toward heaven" (1 Kings 8:54 ESV).

The fourth and fifth are *praying with your head bowed* or *your entire body bowed*: Abraham's servant "bowed his head and worshiped the LORD" (Genesis 24:26 AMP). Ezra's congregants went the extra mile: "Then they bowed down and worshiped the LORD with their faces to the ground" (Nehemiah 8:6 NLT).

The sixth is *praying with your hands lifted*, a position that makes it clear no weapons are in hand. The one praying or praising is in total surrender to their Lord: "I want men to pray with holy hands lifted up to God, free from anger and controversy" (1 Timothy 2:8 NLT).

The seventh is *praying while walking*. That's what Elijah did when he paced back and forth in prayer before bringing a young boy back to life (2 Kings 4:35), not to mention all the psalms of ascent the Israelites sang when ascending the road to Jerusalem to attend various festivals (Psalms 120–134).

Last is *praying while sitting*: "Then King David went in and sat before the LORD and prayed" (1 Chronicles 17:16 NLT).

Perhaps the point is not so much what posture you use when you pray or whether you say your prayers aloud. The main thing is that you pray. That you not neglect this precious gift, this power, this way of relating to God. For nothing happens without prayer.

Rejoice always and delight in your faith; be unceasing and persistent in prayer; in every situation [no matter what the circumstances] be thankful and continually give thanks to God; for this is the will of God for you in Christ Jesus.
1 THESSALONIANS 5:16–18 AMP

Lord, make me a woman of prayer—no matter when, no matter where, no matter how.

Depths of Desire

All told of inward, ardent prayer,
Which Israel's God alone could hear.
And yet the high priest at the shrine
Mistook the prayer for fruits of wine.

After attending the sacrificial feast in Shiloh, the distraught "Hannah got up and went to pray. Eli the priest was sitting at his customary place beside the entrance of the Tabernacle" (1 Samuel 1:9 NLT). In deep anguish, Hannah wept as she prayed silently to the Lord.

This attitude of prayer that Hannah adopted was new. Her lips were moving but no sound came forth. For her prayers were internal, not the usual mode of prayer in those days. George Matheson writes:

> *Men in those days thought that the value of a*
> *petition lay in its words—that they were heard for*
> *their much speaking. . . . A woman who earnestly*
> *moved her lips and said nothing would be looked*
> *upon as in a state of temporary aberration, of*
> *which drink might be the cause.**

The priest Eli, witnessing Hannah and her mode of prayer, thought she was drunk. But Hannah was merely issuing in a new mode of coming before the Lord. In doing so, she was demonstrating her belief that God knows all hearts and their desires. Again, George Matheson writes, "Hannah was before her time in the development of the idea of prayer. She had reached a great truth which the rest of the world waited for, that prayer is simply a wish of the heart directed heavenward, that its potency lies in the depth of the desire."

Hannah went deep. For her desire was deep. Words would not, could not do in her circumstances. She had secret troubles and petitions that she wanted God alone to hear. This was not a public display but a private discussion.

Jesus Himself often slipped away alone to pray to His Father (Mark 1:35; Luke 5:16). Knowing the value of private prayer, He encouraged others to find their own place of prayer, saying, "When you pray, go into your most private room, close the door and pray to your Father who is in secret, and your Father who sees [what is done] in secret will reward you" (Matthew 6:6 AMP). This prayer closet doesn't have to be an actual structure. As with Hannah, it can be a place within you. A place where you alone, in private, in silence, approach God and reveal all your heart's sorrows, concerns, and desires. God will not just honor such prayers but reward you for presenting them in that way!

Today, spend some time in your own prayer closet. Go deep within and reveal to God your heart's deepest desires, knowing He will reward you for these precious private moments.

Rising very early in the morning, while it was still dark, he departed and went out to a desolate place, and there he prayed.
MARK 1:35 ESV

Alone with You, Lord, I bring my heart's deepest desires.

* George Matheson, *The Representative Women of the Bible* (New York: A. C. Armstrong & Son, 1907), 202–3.

Judging the Heart

And while she made the Lord her stay,
He bade her put her cups away.

*a*s Hannah was bowed before the Lord, looking to Him for comfort, strength, and support in spirit, mouthing her silent, heartfelt prayers and petitions, Eli the priest was looking on. Thinking she was intoxicated, he "scolded her, 'How long are you going to be drunk? Get rid of your wine!' " (1 Samuel 1:14 HCSB).

Some scholars say Eli's response was an appropriate reaction to Hannah's mode of prayer, one he'd never witnessed before. Others disagree, saying his judgment was rash and harsh, that we should give others the benefit of the doubt—especially if we hold the godly position of a priest, pastor, or elder.

Perhaps the state of the priesthood and strictures at the tabernacle had decayed to the point where drinking and other disrespectful happenings within the courts of God were becoming commonplace. Perhaps Hannah just seemed to be one more person violating God's laws and decrees. After all, it was still the days of the judges, when "all the people did whatever seemed right in their own eyes" (Judges 21:25 NLT).

Yet the point remains that this minister of God, this man whose own sons, priests themselves, were corrupt, accused this poor-of-spirit yet pure-of-heart woman of having imbibed too much wine at the feast of peace. Would that he would have given her the benefit of the doubt. But he did not.

The irony is that one day God would speak directly to Israel's future priest and judge, Samuel—Hannah's son and the answer to her prayer. And God would make clear to him that "man does not see what the LORD sees, for man sees what is visible, but the LORD sees the heart" (1 Samuel 16:7 HCSB).

Jesus would elaborate on this statement in a remark He made to the religious scholars and officials of His day. "Woe to you. . .hypocrites! For you are like whitewashed tombs, which outwardly appear beautiful, but within are full of dead people's bones and all uncleanness" (Matthew 23:27 ESV).

When it comes to dealing with other people, we must be slow to judge, if we judge at all. For only God knows what is truly in the hearts and souls of others. Thus, we need to "look beneath the surface" (John 7:24 NLT) and stop "looking [only] at the outward appearance of things" (2 Corinthians 10:7 AMP). We must give each other the benefit of the doubt, realizing that our thoughts and judgments might be faulty. For as God reminds us, "My thoughts are not your thoughts, and your ways are not My ways" (Isaiah 55:8 HCSB).

> *"As heaven is higher than earth, so My ways are higher than your ways, and My thoughts than your thoughts."*
> ISAIAH 55:9 HCSB

Help me, Lord, not to be quick to judge, as You alone know the inner workings of each heart.

Hannah's Defense: Part 1

"I am not drunken, O my lord!
I love and fear my Father's word.
Thy handmaid's heart with anguish faints;
I've poured to God my sore complaints."

Imagine finally being able to leave the family dinner table. You take your heavy heart and make your way to a place where you can pray in private. You don't even notice the priest sitting outside the church door.

Alone before God, you pour out your complaints. Through hot and heavy tears, you silently make your petitions known to the Lord, telling Him your deepest wounds and strongest desires. And before you are able to finish your one-on-one time before God, you hear a priest accuse you of being drunk! That was the situation Hannah found herself in. Eli was just one more person adding to her distress. And that one more person was a man of God.

One would think Hannah would have been outraged! That she would have taken this last straw and thrown it back in Eli's face—he whose own sons, priests themselves, were degenerates who disobeyed God's laws and had no faith in their Lord! Hannah easily could have said to him, "Sir, who are you to judge me, to call me a drunk, when you have sons who have no respect for the Lord our God?"

Yet Hannah did not. She merely defended herself, protested her innocence. She told Eli, "No, my lord, I am a woman with a despairing spirit. I have not been drinking wine or any intoxicating drink, but I have poured out my soul before the Lord" (1 Samuel 1:15 AMP).

Bible commentator Matthew Henry writes, "Hannah did not retort the charge, and upbraid Eli with the wicked conduct of his own sons. When we are at any time unjustly censured, we have need to set a double watch before the door of our lips, that we do not return censure for censure. Hannah thought it enough to clear herself, and so must we."*

Hannah was such a wise and patient woman. In a time when she must have been worn raw because of her barrenness, Peninnah's unceasing provocations, Elkanah's inability to understand her heartache, and now Eli's false accusations, she chose to be gracious with her words. Her soft answer and her tamable tongue kept her from being as careless with her words and judgments as Eli was with his.

Would that we could all defend ourselves with a calm heart and gentle manner, putting away all "anger, wrath, malice, slander, and obscene talk" (Colossians 3:8 ESV) from our mouths. For when we do so, we're bound to reap blessings instead of curses.

> *The intelligent person restrains his words, and one who*
> *keeps a cool head is a man of understanding.*
> PROVERBS 17:27 HCSB

> *Lord, help me watch my words, keeping them soft and*
> *anger-free. For in doing so, I know I will be blessed.*

* https://biblehub.com/commentaries/1_samuel/1-12.htm.

Hannah's Defense: Part 2

"Oh no, my lord, strong drink and wine
Have never touched these lips of mine.
Think not thy handmaid e'er should be
One of Belial's company."

annah's first line of defense to Eli's accusation that she was drunk (when in actuality she was just praying silently) was to tell him, "No, my lord, I am a woman of a sorrowful spirit: I have drunk neither wine nor strong drink, but have poured out my soul before the Lᴏʀᴅ" (1 Samuel 1:15 ᴋᴊᴠ). The second statement she made to explain her innocence was "Count not thine handmaid for a daughter of Belial: for out of the abundance of my complaint and grief have I spoken hitherto" (1 Samuel 1:16 ᴋᴊᴠ).

The *Pulpit Commentary* says of Hannah, "She is 'a woman hard of spirit;' heavy hearted. . .and she had been lightening her heart by pouring out her troubles before Jehovah. She is no 'worthless woman;' for Belial is not a proper name, though gradually it became one, but means worthlessness, and 'a daughter of worthlessness' means a bad woman."*

The irony is that the word *Belial* that Hannah uses here to defend herself is later used by the author of the books of Samuel to describe Eli's offspring: "Now the sons of Eli were sons of Belial; they knew not the Lᴏʀᴅ" (1 Samuel 2:12 ᴋᴊᴠ)!

Hannah, the woman pure of heart and soul who was faithful and prayerful, was a far cry from the likes of Eli's sons and other worthless characters—such as Nabal—who were linked to the term *Belial* (1 Samuel 25:25; 2 Samuel 20:1; 1 Kings 21:10).

What an example Hannah sets before us. Her faith and devotion to God were so strong that she could rise above any misunderstandings and misjudgments from a man who was Israel's highest spiritual leader! A lowly woman, a handmaiden of the Lord, Hannah had the courage to stand up to the unjust remarks of Eli, and to do so coolly and calmly.

There will be times when just as we're giving our best selves to the Lord, those from whom we expect encouragement will seek to discourage us. Consider how Judas criticized Mary of Bethany when she poured a pound of perfume upon Jesus' feet, wiping them with her hair. Judas complained to Jesus that what she'd done was a waste of money, yet Jesus defended her actions. Immediately after that passage, a crowd of unbelievers wanted not just to discourage but to kill the resurrected Lazarus "because he was the reason many of the Jews were deserting them and believing in Jesus" (John 12:11 HCSB).

When you're following the Lord's path, never lose heart. Keep doing good, and you will find yourself in the best of company: Jesus'.

*We must not get tired of doing good, for we will
reap at the proper time if we don't give up.*
GALATIANS 6:9 HCSB

Walking Your way, Lord, I will never lose heart.

* https://biblehub.com/commentaries/1_samuel/1-12.htm.

Poured Out

"Oppressed with grief, a heavy load,
I've poured my soul in prayer to God."

In her intense distress and weariness of heart and soul, Hannah was driven to seek the only One who could truly understand her and help her: the Lord of Hosts. F. B. Meyer writes:

> *The grief of the childless wife drove Hannah to*
> *God. There she found her only resource. When the*
> *heart is nigh to breaking, what else can we do than*
> *pour out our complaint before the One who is ever*
> *ready to hear our cry? We may trust God with*
> *our secrets; He will keep sacred our confidence.*
> *Elkanah's love may go a long way, but we have*
> *for the most part to tread the wine-press alone.*
> *After we have eaten and drunk before our friends,*
> *"anointing our head and washing our face," that*
> *they may not guess what is happening within, we*
> *must have a spot where we can unbend and open*
> *the sluice-gates of grief. And what place is so good*
> *as the Mercy-Seat?**

You may think your nearest and dearest are your best avenues of support, ones who will listen without interrupting, let you cry on their shoulder, help you find a way through the dark valleys we all experience at one time or another in our lives. But only God can heal a broken heart (Psalm 147:3). Only God can listen to you pour out your soul and not interrupt but hold you until you've shed your last tear, uttered your last groan. Only God will give you the exact advice you need or lead you to a solution you never could have imagined.

How do we know this? Because God told us. And He never lies (Numbers 23:19).

God wants you to know that when your heart is broken and your spirit crushed, He is near (Psalm 34:18). He is the One who is always with you, ready to strengthen you, help you, and hold you up (Isaiah 41:10). For He is love. When He is in your life, in your prayer closet, He will listen patiently to everything you have to say, then shower you with His peace and love (John 3:16; 14:27).

When there are secrets you can only share with God, go to Him. Open up your "sluice-gates of grief" and pour out all your sorrows. Trust Him to keep all your secret petitions close to His heart. Encourage and strengthen yourself in Him (1 Samuel 30:6), knowing that He will respond, He will give you guidance (verses 7–8), and He will grant you success (verses 18–20) above all that you ever hoped, dreamed, or imagined.

> *Trust [confidently] in Him at all times, O people; pour out your heart before Him. God is a refuge for us.*
> PSALM 62:8 AMP

> *Lord God, my Refuge and Friend, I come to You, pouring out my heart, telling You all.*

* *F. B. Meyer Bible Commentary* (Wheaton, IL: Tyndale House, 1979), 117.

Blessing 1: Peace

"Daughter of Israel! go in peace.
May all thy griefs and sorrows cease."

Eli the priest had accused the praying Hannah of being drunk. As she offers up an explanation, he quietly listens to her defense. Hannah says she is not one who drinks wine, just a troubled woman who is pouring out her heart and soul to God.

Giving credit where credit is due, Eli not only quickly realizes his mistake but kindly and nobly blesses her with his next three words: "Go in peace" (1 Samuel 1:17 NIV).

Here we have a man who has spoken in error, blaming an innocent woman of being drunk, but who quickly seeks to make up for his unjust accusation. By humbly praying Hannah go in peace, Eli forgets himself, his own pride, seeking to lift her up and lifting himself up in Hannah's eyes in the process.

Would that more of us would be like Eli, quick to admit our error and rectify whatever injustice we have meted out. How often do we take a line of belief, an opinion that we later find to be wrong, and refuse to back down from that opinion? Soon we find ourselves stubbornly sticking to everything we say as if it's God's honest truth, when deep down we realize it is not. Or how often do we shut out the words of others, refusing to give them any credence because we are too prideful to admit we may have made a mistake or jumped to the wrong conclusion?

God must have been smiling down on this scene between this priest and this woman. The former may have had trouble keeping his sons on the straight and narrow. But here he seems to say just the right thing at just the right time to repair whatever damage his careless words may have inflicted upon a woman already in deep despair.

In one of his letters, Paul gives us some advice for keeping the peace with others and with God. He tells us to be humble, gentle, and "patient with each other, making allowance for each other's faults" (Ephesians 4:2 NLT). We who have learned about Jesus are to throw off our old selves and put on the new, allowing the Holy Spirit to renew our thoughts, desires, and attitudes (Ephesians 4:20–24). That means not getting angry, as well as letting "everything you say be good and helpful, so that your words will be an encouragement to those who hear them" (Ephesians 4:29 NLT).

Today, watch your words. Make sure you are speaking in tones of love. When you mess up, admit you have made a mistake. Be a humble woman of peace and love. And you will find yourself being a blessing—to yourself, others, and God.

God has called us to peace.
1 CORINTHIANS 7:15 AMP

Lord, make me a woman of peace, blessed by peace.

Blessing 2: Heart's Desire

"May God with hope thy heart inspire,
And grant thee all thy heart's desire."

The second part of the priest Eli's blessing to the woman he had earlier unjustly maligned is "May the God of Israel grant the request you have asked of him" (1 Samuel 1:17 NLT). Whether this was a prayer or prophecy we do not know. But that the high priest bestowed this blessing upon God's humble handmaiden is amazing!

Perhaps Eli, having listened carefully with his ears and heart to Hannah's defense, was struck with the realization that here was a woman who had surrendered her will and her soul totally to God. George Matheson writes, "She hopes. . .that she will receive an answer to her prayer; but the *music* of the hope lies in the fact that it will be *God's* answer. She would not desire the privileges of the home if it were not for the sake of building a house for God. Her attitude is purely sacrificial."*

When the desires of our hearts are aligned with the kingdom of God, we will receive what we ask for. That's a promise made by Jesus in John 15:7 (AMP): "If you remain in Me and My words remain in you [that is, if we are vitally united and My message lives in your heart], ask whatever you wish and it will be done for you."

Perhaps you have been praying for something, hoping for a desire of your heart to be answered, established, satisfied. You have read how God grants such requests, verses like "Take delight in the LORD, and He will give you your heart's desires" (Psalm 37:4 HCSB); "May he grant your heart's desires and make all your plans succeed" (Psalm 20:4 NLT); and "For you have given him his heart's desire;

you have withheld nothing he requested" (Psalm 21:2 NLT). You have prayed and prayed and prayed. But you have yet to see God answer your prayer. Perhaps the hitch is that your request or your attitude linked to your request is more in line with your *own* wants and will than with God's.

Hannah had asked God for a son. A son she would then give back to God. That is a sacrificial request. That is a woman offering herself, her life, her future up to God, telling Him in no uncertain terms that she is a vessel for His use. This is a woman who has spent some quality time with God—even in the days of the judges when "all the people did whatever seemed right in their own eyes" (Judges 21:25 NLT).

Today, link up to Jesus. And ask Him to help you realign the desires of your heart.

The heart of man plans his way, but the LORD establishes his steps.
PROVERBS 16:9 ESV

Dear Lord, help me discern the true desires of my heart.

* George Matheson, *The Representative Women of the Bible* (New York: A. C. Armstrong & Son, 1907), 206–7.

Pray On!

The supplicant has cast her care
On God, who hears and answers prayer.

*C*onsider all the challenges Hannah has been facing in the first seventeen verses of 1 Samuel.

Her husband, Elkanah, had two wives: Hannah and Peninnah. The second wife had children but the first did not. And each year that Elkanah and his family went to Shiloh to sacrifice to the Lord, Peninnah would tease Hannah unmercifully.

Elkanah, who loved and favored Hannah, always gave her a double portion of the sacrifice because she was barren. His obvious favoritism only served to fuel Peninnah's ire against Hannah. Her taunts would bring Hannah to tears, causing her to lose her appetite.

Elkanah asked Hannah, "Why are you crying? . . . Why won't you eat? Why are you troubled? Am I not better to you than 10 sons?" (1 Samuel 1:8 HCSB). Yet these words brought little comfort to Hannah. She knew where she needed to go, whom she needed to seek: God in the tent of meeting.

After dinner, Hannah got up and made her way to the tabernacle. Eli the priest, sitting at the entrance, saw her in her deep anguish and sorrow, praying to God as she wept. She made a silent vow to God, praying, "O LORD of Heaven's Armies, if you will look upon my sorrow and answer my prayer and give me a son, then I will give him back to you. He will be yours for his entire lifetime, and as a sign that he has been dedicated to the LORD, his hair will never be cut" (1 Samuel 1:11 NLT). But the next thing she knew, the high priest was accusing her of being drunk! About Hannah's tenacity, F. B. Meyer writes:

> *Many were coming and going in the Tabernacle-court. It was no place for private prayer; and this sad woman had no opportunity for audible petition, so she spake in her heart. We may all do that amid the crowds that sweep gaily past us in their light-hearted way. Let us not grow weary. "She continued praying before the Lord." People may misunderstand and reproach you. The Eli's that judge superficially may leap to hasty conclusions, but pray on! Pray on, though the prayer seem impossible of answer! Pray on, though heart and flesh fail! Pray on, for God will yet raise the poor from the dust and the beggar from the dunghill! When you have committed your cause to God, go in peace and be no more sad.* *

No matter what came up against Hannah, she never gave up. And neither should you. No matter what, get yourself to God. Allow no distractions, noise, or comments of others to dissuade you from your purpose. Continue praying no matter how impossible your petition may seem. Pray on. Pray on.

> *Jesus told his disciples a story to show that they should always pray and never give up.*
> LUKE 18:1 NLT

To You, Lord, I pray on.

* F. B. Meyer Bible Commentary (Wheaton, IL: Tyndale House, 1979), 117.

Unburden

And now her cross is borne by Him
Who sits between the cherubim. . . .

Hannah had come to God, had met with Him at His tent. With tears streaming down her face, she had poured out her heart to Him. Soon afterward, she'd been first reprimanded and then blessed by Eli the high priest.

Perhaps having to defend herself against Eli's judgments had allowed her to review and realize what she'd just done: "I've been pouring out my heart before the Lord. . . . I've been praying from the depth of my anguish and resentment" (1 Samuel 1:15–16 HCSB). And who she'd been when she'd done it: "I am a woman with a broken heart. . . . Don't think of me as a wicked woman" (verses 15–16 HCSB).

It wasn't that Hannah had changed physically. Not yet, anyway. It was that she had just been able to finally put down the huge burden she'd been carrying all these years. And now that it had slid off her shoulders and landed at God's feet, her problem was now His.

Hannah had done what Psalm 55:22 (AMP) encourages: "Cast your burden on the Lord [release it] and He will sustain and uphold you; He will never allow the righteous to be shaken (slip, fall, fail)." She had finally let everything go, giving her burden to the Lord who would bear it and who also "daily bears *us* up" (Psalm 68:19 ESV, emphasis added).

Hannah must have felt a bit like the woman who was so bent over that she couldn't straighten up at all, having been "disabled by a spirit for over 18 years" (Luke 13:11 HCSB). Although bent double, this woman, like Hannah, persevered in attending God's house. She did not allow her infirmity, her troubles, her woes to keep her from seeking God's presence.

Jesus was in the synagogue teaching when He saw the bent-over woman and immediately cried out, " 'Woman you are free of your disability.' Then He laid His hands on her, and instantly she was restored and began to glorify God" (Luke 13:12–13 HCSB).

Might we all find our troubles impelling us to God's house to seek His presence, His face, His solace, His strength. Too often we allow our troubles to repel us from God's house and from God Himself. Perhaps we're embarrassed to let others see us so heartbroken. Yet if we listen closely, that's just our pride talking.

The humble Jesus teaches us that we're going to have a hard road ahead, even though we are His people, His followers (John 16:33). But He is here to help us, to give us rest and relief from the weariness of our heavy burdens (Matthew 11:28). So don't wait. Let go of your pride. Embrace your humility and take your broken heart, your load of troubles to the One who heals us and bears our burdens.

"Now I will take the load from your shoulders."
PSALM 81:6 NLT

Lord, ease this burden from my back, I pray!

New Strength

And Hannah leaves the throne of grace
With glory shining in her face.

H annah unloaded all her troubles and dropped them at God's feet. He now knows, from her very lips, her heartbreaking situation. Afterward Hannah left His throne of grace with a light step, a shining face, and a bright smile.

What miracle wrought such a change in our heroine? No miracle, really. Just the *certainty* that the God of miracles, the Lord of Hosts, had heard Hannah's prayer. Her troubles, dreams, and desires were now in the best place possible—God's hands. And if anyone could rescue her from her present situation, surely the Lord who sat on the throne of grace would do so.

Yet that's not all! In her time with God, Hannah received new strength. And she did so by admitting her lowliness.

In Hannah's prayer to the Lord, in the vow she made to Him, three times she referred to herself as God's handmaid, maidservant, or servant: "O LORD of hosts, if you will indeed look on the affliction of your *servant* and remember me and not forget your *servant*, but will give to your *servant* a son, then I will give him to the LORD all the days of his life, and no razor shall touch his head" (1 Samuel 1:11 ESV, emphasis added). She admitted to God (and perhaps to herself) her humility, surrender to, and dependence upon Him. And in doing so, Hannah found her strength renewed.

When we allow ourselves to give all our dreams and desires to the Lord, knowing they are not something we can obtain by ourselves, God is pleased. That's when He will turn His attention to us, hear us, and move on our behalf. That is what He promises in 2 Chronicles 7:14 (NLT): "If my people who are called by my name will humble themselves and pray and seek my face and turn from their wicked ways, I will hear from heaven and will forgive their sins and restore their land." It's one of God's if-then promises. We must move first—humbling ourselves, praying and seeking God's face, turning from our sins. Then God will move—hearing from heaven, forgiving our sins, and restoring us to Himself.

Yet God will not just restore those who humble themselves before Him. He will also lift them up (Psalm 147:6). He will save them (Job 22:29). He will give them the kingdom of heaven (Matthew 5:3).

The next time you present yourself to God, have true humility in your heart. Willingly surrender to Him all you are and hope for. Admit you are completely dependent upon Him. And you too will leave the throne of grace with glory shining in your face and strength welling up in your heart.

"God is opposed to the proud and haughty, but
[continually] gives [the gift of] grace to the humble
[who turn away from self-righteousness]."
JAMES 4:6 AMP

I come to You as Your lowly servant,
Lord, surrendering my all to You.

Transformation

And now she moves on holy ground,
Diffusing heavenly sweetness round.

Weeping, Hannah entered the throne room of God with a heavy heart and a troubled mind. There at God's feet she admitted her weakness and her sorrows. She told God how she had been abused because of her barrenness and how she had longed for a child. She humbly offered herself as a vessel to be used by God, a vessel to bring a son into the world, one whom she might cherish for a few years and then give back to God for His own desires and purposes. Hannah surrendered herself and her problems, left them in God's hands, then arose transformed.

Having walked into the tent that housed God's presence feeling cursed, she came out blessed. Praying in her weakness, she was given strength. Humbled at His feet, she rose with an uplifted heart.

God has an amazing way of transforming us when we seek Him, linger in His presence, open our hearts to His examination, and offer ourselves to Him. We come to Him weak, and He tells us we can be strong (2 Corinthians 12:9–10; Philippians 4:13). He tells us that we who are defeated can have victory in our lives (1 Corinthians 15:57). That we who are lost will be found (Luke 15:6–7). That we who feel worthless are valuable in God's eyes (Matthew 10:29–31). That we who have done wrong will be made right (Psalm 103:10–18). That we who are anxious will find peace (Philippians 4:6–7). That we who mourn will not only find comfort but comfort others (Matthew 5:4; 2 Corinthians 1:3–5). That we who feel unloved or unlovable are loved (Ephesians 3:17–19). That we who are alone will find a family (Psalm 68:6). That we who are in chains will discover freedom (John 8:36). And God does this transformative work every time we go to Him for help, forgiveness, deliverance, and wisdom.

Moreover, when God does transform those of us who believe, other people notice. For we give off a scent of sweetness, a heavenly fragrance. God then "uses us to spread the knowledge of Christ everywhere, like a sweet perfume" (2 Corinthians 2:14 NLT).

Today, allow yourself to be transformed. Go to God. Enter His throne room. Unload your troubles. Ask for His help. Surrender all you have and are to His use. And He will transform you (Ezekiel 36:26), giving you a new heart and spirit; He will make you a new creation (2 Corinthians 5:17). And you will arise smelling sweet.

I pray that your hearts will be flooded with light so that you can understand the confident hope he has given to those he called—his holy people who are his rich and glorious inheritance.
EPHESIANS 1:18 NLT

I surrender myself to Your transformative powers, Lord. Mold me into the woman You created me to be.

Believing Prayer

Such joys believing prayer imparts
To weary minds and bleeding hearts.

Hannah rose from prayer certain God had heard all she revealed to Him. After being unjustly accused by Eli, she was then blessed with his words "Go in peace, and may the God of Israel grant the petition you've requested from Him" (1 Samuel 1:17 HCSB). Hannah replied, "Let your servant find favor in your eyes" (verse 18 ESV). Then she went on her way, ate some of her dinner, and actually smiled! That's the effect that belief in the power of prayer has on a person.

David knew that power. In one verse, he asserts to himself what he believes God will do for him, praises God, and then ends with a prayer: "The LORD will fulfill His purpose for me. LORD, Your love is eternal; do not abandon the work of Your hands" (Psalm 138:8 HCSB).

Perhaps that's what made David so successful. He was in a perpetual loop of belief in God, praise of God, and prayer to God. That sounds like a great place to be! For that is not only how we are instructed to pray but also the pathway to joy and peace.

Consider Philippians 4:4, 6–7 (NLT):

> *Always be full of joy in the Lord. I say it again—*
> *rejoice! . . . Don't worry about anything; instead,*
> *pray about everything. Tell God what you need,*
> *and thank him for all he has done. Then you will*
> *experience God's peace, which exceeds anything we*
> *can understand. His peace will guard your hearts*
> *and minds as you live in Christ Jesus.*

Our pathway to peace, our weapon against worry, our antidote to angst is to do what Hannah did! To not worry about *any*thing and to pray about *every*thing. To reveal to God every little secret we are harboring in our hearts.

We are then to lay down our burdens at God's feet—and leave them there! We're not just to give Him a laundry list of what we need but to thank Him for all He's already given us. Only then will we have the joy we seek, the peace we crave.

Once we leave God's presence, we're not to look back at what we've left behind but to forget about the troubles that have weighed us down, looking away from all those things that distract our minds and bring fear into our hearts. We're to keep our eyes on God, our minds on praiseworthy things, believing He knows and will fulfill our deepest desires.

Practice these things [in daily life], and the God [who is the source] of peace and well-being will be with you.
PHILIPPIANS 4:9 AMP

Thank You, Lord, for all You have done,
will do, and are doing in my life! Amen!

Morning Devotions

At early dawn the household rise
And worship God with sacrifice;
And as in praise and prayer they bow. . .

Even in the evil days of judges, Elkanah and his family held the Lord in reverence. For in the early morning hours, his entire household rose and worshipped God before the long trek back to their home (1 Samuel 1:19). How pious, how earnest in their worship of God, were Hannah and her family.

About this portion of Hannah's story, Bible commentator Matthew Henry writes:

> *Elkanah and his family had a journey before them,*
> *and a family of children to take with them, yet*
> *they would not move till they had worshipped God*
> *together. Prayer and provender do not hinder a*
> *journey. When men are in such haste to set out*
> *upon journeys, or to engage in business, that they*
> *have not time to worship God, they are likely to*
> *proceed without his presence and blessing.**

Jacob hastily began a journey to his mother's family after he'd tricked his father into giving him the elder brother's blessing. That night, Jacob dreamed of a ladder with angels descending and ascending upon it. God spoke to Jacob in that dream, revealing that all people would be blessed through him. God then comforted him by telling him, "I am with you and will watch over you wherever you go.

I will bring you back to this land, for I will not leave you until I have done what I have promised you" (Genesis 28:15 HCSB). Early the next morning, Jacob, realizing God was in that place, set up a pillar to worship God and mark the spot of his vision (Genesis 28:18).

Job, whenever his children would end a period of feasting, would get up early the next morning and sacrifice a burnt offering for each child, just in case his sons "sinned and cursed God in their hearts" (Job 1:5 AMP).

Even (and perhaps especially) when he was in the wilderness, running from Saul, David sought God with the dawn (Psalm 57:8).

Jesus Himself maintained the practice of seeking God early. Mark 1:35 (NLT) says, "Before daybreak the next morning, Jesus got up and went out to an isolated place to pray."

By adhering to an early morning practice of devotional time with God, you'll be ensuring He will be a conscious part of your day, not something you brush to the side and include in your day *if* you can squeeze Him in.

If you don't already seek God early, try starting such a practice today. Journal what changes take place when you make God your first priority. Meeting with Him at the beginning of the day will make all the difference in the world, above and below.

I rise before dawn and cry out for help; I put my hope in Your word.
PSALM 119:147 HCSB

I come to You amid the morning light, Lord.
Hear my prayer and praise.

* https://biblehub.com/commentaries/1_samuel/1-19.htm.

Sacred Rites

And holier feelings rule and reign,
As they approach their home again.
So sacred rites are wisely given,
To aid us to our home in heaven.

We can see that Hannah and Elkanah had the right mindset and attitude when they practiced their sacred rites at the tabernacle. Perhaps not so much Peninnah, whose behavior toward Hannah as they traveled to and from Shiloh proved to be reprehensible, the kind of behavior of which the God of love would not approve.

Jesus Himself took issue with those who trusted in their traditions and practices. They considered themselves good people, right with God because of their religious routines, thinking those rituals—performed with the head, not the heart—would commend them to God. Jesus told the parable of the Pharisee and the tax collector who went to the temple to pray. The Pharisee stood and prayed, "I thank you, God, that I am not like other people—cheaters, sinners, adulterers. I'm certainly not like that tax collector! I fast twice a week, and I give you a tenth of my income" (Luke 18:11–12 NLT).

Then the tax collector, who would not even lift his eyes up to heaven as he prayed but beat his chest in grief, said, "O God, be merciful to me, for I am a sinner" (Luke 18:13 NLT).

Jesus' point? The ones who are humble in heart before God are the ones who will become right with God and lifted up, not those who exalt themselves above all others.

The problem is some religious people don't see themselves as needing to put any heart into their relationship with God. They simply perform the same old rites and practices, then go about their day behaving as if they are God's gift to humankind, above all others, needing no one and nothing, including a heart-to-heart relationship with their Rescuer!

Consider when Jesus visited a Pharisee named Simon. While Jesus sat at the table, an immoral woman from the city washed His feet with her tears and her hair, "kissing them and anointing them with the fragrant oil" (Luke 7:38 HCSB).

The Pharisee, witnessing her actions, abhorred them, saying, "If this man was the prophet I thought he was, he would have known what kind of woman this is who is falling all over him" (Luke 7:39 MSG). But Jesus rose to her defense, saying that since He'd entered Simon's house, the latter had given Him no water for His feet. But this woman had ministered to Him by anointing them with her perfume, washing them with her tears, and wiping them with her hair. And because she did this, loving Him so much from her heart, she would be forgiven much.

Today, consider your own religious rites and routines, and resolve to perform them from your heart rather than your head.

What is important is faith expressing itself in love.
GALATIANS 5:6 NLT

Lord, I come to You now, seeking You with all the love in my heart.

Remembered by God

There's rest in Ramah. God bestows
A healing balm for Hannah's woes.

lkanah and his family have left the tabernacle at Shiloh and returned home to Ramah. There "Elkanah was intimate with his wife Hannah, and the LORD remembered her" (1 Samuel 1:19 HCSB). God remembered her problem, her heartfelt desire, her vow. And on these things He moved.

God acted in Hannah's life just as He did in the life of the childless Sarah: "The LORD graciously remembered and visited Sarah as He had said, and the LORD did for her as He had promised. So Sarah conceived and gave birth to a son for Abraham in his old age" (Genesis 21:1–2 AMP). God acted, remembering a barren Rachel as well: "God remembered [the prayers of] Rachel, and God thought of her and opened her womb [so that she would conceive]. So she conceived and gave birth to a son" (Genesis 30:22–23 AMP).

Why wouldn't God act on behalf of His daughters? This is the God who tells us, "Can a woman forget her nursing child, or lack compassion for the child of her womb? Even if these forget, yet I will not forget you. Look, I have inscribed you on the palms of My hands" (Isaiah 49:15–16 HCSB)!

Not only are you tattooed on the palms of God's hands, but He is with you wherever you go (Joshua 1:9). Because He is your Shepherd, you will never want for anything but will be led by still waters, refreshed in green pastures, restored in your soul; His rod and His staff will be with you to comfort you, protect you, guide you (Psalm 23).

Just as God remembered Noah and made the waters subside (Genesis 8:1), He will never ever leave you hanging out to dry. He has a plan, a grand plan, and you are a part of it. So know that God remembers. Keep the faith, "the assurance of things hoped for, the conviction of things not seen" (Hebrews 11:1 ESV), knowing God has heard your prayer and will remember you, do for you, when the time is right, in accordance with His timetable.

God remembers all the things He's done, the promises He's made (1 Chronicles 16:12). Yet something He won't remember are your sins, your missteps. Those He promises to blot out of existence (Isaiah 43:25; Hebrews 10:17).

So keep the faith. Draw near to God. And while you're there, do your own remembering. Remind yourself that God is real and rewards those who look to Him and seek Him out (Hebrews 11:6). Then when God does remember you, be like Hannah, standing in the spot where you once offered your prayer and praising Him for His answer (1 Samuel 1:24–2:10)!

> *He's GOD, our God, in charge of the whole earth. And he*
> *remembers, remembers his Covenant—for a thousand*
> *generations he's been as good as his word.*
> PSALM 105:8 MSG

Thank You, Lord, for remembering, for keeping Your Word!

Fruitful Prayers

There's joy in Ramah. Hannah bears
A son, the fruit of many prayers.

After years of sorrow, Hannah gives birth to a child—a son! What a celebration that must have been! In her hands she held the proof that God answers prayer. Her humility, her faithfulness, her constancy, her belief that God would somehow work a miracle through her was rewarded.

God has a history of answering prayer above and beyond what has been requested, especially the prayers of those who seek God early and humble themselves before Him.

Consider Jehoshaphat, king of Judah. He'd been told that three great armies were coming to attack him, his city, and his people. Frightened, he "set himself [determinedly, as his vital need] to seek the Lord; and he proclaimed a fast throughout all Judah" (2 Chronicles 20:3 AMP). In response, his people came together to seek help from God, "longing for Him with all their heart" (verse 4 AMP).

Then King Jehoshaphat stood among his people in God's temple and prayed, admitting his weakness: "We are powerless against this great multitude which is coming against us. We do not know what to do, but our eyes are on You" (verse 12 AMP). Humble words such as these, especially coming from a king, touch God's heart, prompting Him to do a great work on the petitioner's behalf.

Through a prophet, God answered Jehoshaphat's prayer, saying:

> *"Be not afraid or dismayed at this great multitude,*
> *for the battle is not yours, but God's. . . . You need*

not fight in this battle; take your positions, stand
and witness the salvation of the LORD who is with
you, O Judah and Jerusalem. Do not fear or be
dismayed; tomorrow go out against them, for the
LORD is with you." (verses 15, 17 AMP)

In response, showing his extreme humility, "Jehoshaphat bowed with his face to the ground, and all Judah and the inhabitants of Jerusalem fell down before the LORD, worshiping Him" (verse 18 AMP).

Jehoshaphat followed God's orders. He encouraged his people, telling them, "Believe and trust in the LORD your God and you will be established (secure). Believe and trust in His prophets and succeed" (verse 20 AMP). He then sent the praise singers ahead of his army. As their voices filled the air, God worked so that the enemy armies turned against each other. In the end, all Jehoshaphat and his people had to do was take all the spoil the armies had left behind.

May you be as humble a pray-er as Hannah and Jehoshaphat, following the Lord's instructions and believing in His Word. Then you too will be reaping the fruit of your prayers!

When they call on me, I will answer. . . . I will rescue and honor them.
PSALM 91:15 NLT

Lord, I come to You on my knees. Hear my plea. . . .

God's Gift

And as her soft glad eyes behold
The precious child her arms infold,
She owns the gift is from above,
The pledge of God's approving love.

Imagine Hannah's delight. Her prayers to God have been answered. She holds in her arms a precious child (1 Samuel 1:20), proof that God is the miracle worker, that He does answer the prayers of those He loves!

She and the proud papa Elkanah count their child's fingers and toes. Exultant with joy, they look into the eyes of the proof of their love and thank God for the gift with which He has blessed them. A gift that they know will one day have to be returned.

This knowledge must have been difficult for both parents, but especially for Hannah. For she doesn't know if she will be able to bear any more children. This may be her one and only child, the only babe she will hold close to her heart, nurse from her breast, sing softly to sleep, and teach to walk and talk.

The brave and courageous Hannah is teaching us that our "children are a gift from the LORD; they are a reward from him" (Psalm 127:3 NLT). And that gift, that reward, is a temporary one. For every day a child grows further and further away from us.

Once a child has been delivered from the womb and into the world, he goes through different stages of growth. First, he moves his head from side to side. Then he holds up his neck and head while on his belly. Next, he reaches out and grabs at objects, pushes up on his arms while on his belly, rolls over, and eventually crawls. Soon the child is walking, then running, first to us, then away from us.

Even though that is the natural order of things, somehow we are always caught by surprise when our children reach young adulthood and move out. We wonder where the years have gone and how we'll get along without them. We grieve over how quiet our home has become. And then we remember that someday our children may have children of their own! And the gifting from God starts all over again!

Today, thank God for the gift of children in your family or church. Remember they are only on loan from God. And do your best to love them and reward them, just as God loves and rewards you.

*Every good gift and every perfect gift is from above,
coming down from the Father of lights, with whom
there is no variation or shadow due to change.*
JAMES 1:17 ESV

---

*Lord, thank You for rewarding me with children—those I
have borne and those You have put in my care as a teacher,
leader, fellow believer. Help me to remember children are
a temporary gift from You. Then give me the strength to
love and reward them as You love and reward me.*

What's in a Name?

His name is Samuel: precious word,
Because she asked him of the Lord.

Most likely with Elkanah's approval, Hannah called her new son "Samuel, for she said, 'I have asked for him from the LORD' " (1 Samuel 1:20 ESV).

Among the early Hebrews, children were given their names sometimes by their fathers and other times by their mothers (Genesis 4:1, 26; 5:28–29; 19:37; 21:3). On at least seven occasions, children—Ishmael, Isaac, Solomon, Josiah, Cyrus, John the Baptist, and Jesus (Genesis 16:11; 17:19; 1 Chronicles 22:9; 1 Kings 13:2; Isaiah 45:1–7; Luke 1:13; 1:30–33)—were named by God before they had even come into the world! And those names meant something special.

The name *Samuel* means either "asked of God" or "heard God." Both seem to fit this babe. For this was the child the once-barren Hannah had "asked of God." The one she had vowed, if given to her, would be raised as a Nazirite (Numbers 6) and given back to God.

"Heard God" is also an excellent name for Samuel, who would become a great prophet and priest. It also points to what we learn about Samuel when he is a young child in the high priest Eli's care.

At that time, it was rare to hear the word of the Lord (1 Samuel 3:1). Yet when Eli and Samuel were lying down near each other in the tabernacle of God, the Lord called Samuel. Thinking Eli was speaking, Samuel ran to the priest and said, "Here I am, for you called me" (verse 5 ESV). Eli told Samuel he hadn't called him and bade him lie back down. This happened two more times before Eli realized God must have been calling Samuel. So Eli told him, "Go, lie down, and if he calls you, you shall say, 'Speak, LORD, for your servant hears' " (verse 9 ESV). Samuel listened to Eli, did as instructed, and then heard his first message from God.

This account is a reminder to keep ourselves open to the voice of God. To not just continually bombard Him with our troubles and tears and then walk away. But to come before Him ready to open our ears, mind, heart, and spirit to His voice and to wait for a response. When was the last time you sat down to pray, gave up all that was burdening you, submitted your requests, and then said to God, "Speak, Lord, for Your servant hears"?

Jesus is standing right now at the door of your heart, knocking. Listen for His voice. Open the door. And be all ears as you spend time in His presence.

"Look! I stand at the door and knock. If you hear my voice and open the door, I will come in, and we will share a meal together as friends."
REVELATION 3:20 NLT

Here I am, Lord. Speak! I, Your servant, am listening!

Temporary

That name, when spoken, will impart
Sweet lessons to the mother's heart.

Hannah had named her child Asked of God. Every time she said his name, she was reminded that he was an answer to prayer. That God had blessed her by bringing her one great desire—to conceive and birth another being—to fruition. At the same time, Asked of God must have reminded Hannah of her vow to her Lord, one her selfless heart had willingly offered. Somewhere in the back of her mind, she understood that sometime soon she would have to give up this precious child, give him back to the God from whom he came.

Hannah had two choices. She could allow Asked of God's name to catch in her throat each time she said it because it reminded her she would have to give him back to God. Or she could allow herself to glory in that name because God had made good on His promise, just as she would soon make good on hers. She could choose to make these precious moments with her child something to savor, and so remain unaffected by any anxiety over what would happen in the future. She could decide that what she had in her life in each minute was enough to celebrate in that minute.

Imagine you had a magnificent answer to one of your own greatest desires, and you named that answer Asked of God. Every time you looked at it, your heart swelled with joy. Yet sometimes you became anxious, hoping this answer, this thing you Asked of God, would never be taken from you.

We'd do well to remember that everything we have comes from God's hand (Psalm 145:16). That all we see around us is something

He created and blessed the world with. And that all these things, these gifts that have come from His hand, whether specifically requested or not, are temporary. Changeable. Impermanent. Just as we are.

People change. Desires change. Requests change. Answers change. They may be here one day and gone the next. Yet that is not what we are to focus on. For God would have us just find joy in each of our days, not worrying about what will happen if a particular person or thing ends up out of our reach or out of existence altogether.

Today, look at all you have and are, all you've asked for and all you've been blessed with, and thank God for it. Instead of being attached to or concerned with earthly things that will one day be dust, focus on Him. And on the things that are in heaven, not upon the earth (Colossians 3:1). Make a point every morning of saying to yourself and those you love:

This is the day that the LORD has made; let us rejoice and be glad in it.
PSALM 118:24 ESV

Amen!

The Key Player

How God was moved to hear the cry
She uttered in her agony:
And how her soul was called to raise
To heaven adoring love and praise.

Hannah, in naming her baby Samuel or "Asked of God," pointed clearly to the Maker and Shaker in her life, in this birth, in this gift. She recognized within her heart and made it known to the world that God was the key player in her story.

Hannah, a devout woman of godly character, had been beyond sad. And she'd known of only one person to whom she could go for help, comfort, and relief: the Creator of the universe.

Elkanah, her husband, also a devout follower of God, took her to Yahweh's tabernacle in Shiloh. From His feast table she rose. Once within the courtyard of His tabernacle, she got down on her knees. Before Him she humbled herself.

To Yahweh she submitted. Into His ears she poured out her complaints. To Him she lifted up her voice and committed her vow. If Yahweh would take notice of her and remember her, if He would give her a son, she would raise him as a Nazirite and give him back to God. Eli, the high priest, gave her reassurance that God would answer her prayer, would fulfill her request, because he spoke on Yahweh's behalf.

Yahweh was moved when He heard the account Hannah related, the petition she prayed, the tears she cried. So He moved on her behalf. And when Hannah and Elkanah got home, Yahweh remembered her. Eventually, she gave birth to a son. And with her son in her arms, she couldn't help but lift her voice in praise and adoration of her Yahweh.

The Lord of Hosts holds the key in *all* our stories. As He did for Hannah, He will do for us—if we humble ourselves, make requests in accordance with our desires and His will, and believe we will receive what we've asked.

Charles Spurgeon said, "Prayer bends the omnipotence of heaven to your desire. Prayer moves the hand that moves the world." If you want God to be the key player in your life and not just someone who makes an occasional cameo appearance, humble yourself before Him. Tell Him all your troubles. Offer up your petition within His will. Then rise from your knees and go on your way, believing your prayer will be answered. And knowing your praises to Him will be on your lips when it is.

I am certain that I will see the Lord's goodness in the land of the living. Wait for the Lord; be strong and courageous. Wait for the Lord.
PSALM 27:13–14 HCSB

Lord, I pray I would make You the key player in my life.

Loving Support

The year rolls round. To Shiloh's court
The holy tribes of God resort.
To Shiloh's court, the place of prayer,
Elkanah and his house repair;
Before the mercy seat to bow,
And worship God, and pay his vow.

a year had passed since Elkanah and his family had traveled to Shiloh to worship God. And since a heart-weary and soul-withered Hannah had sought God's refuge to release her tears and made her vows before Him, pleading for a son.

Now it was time for Elkanah and his family to make the trip to Shiloh again. But things had changed. Hannah had given birth to Samuel. And she doesn't want to accompany her family on this trip, instead wanting to wait until her child is weaned before she turns him over to God (1 Samuel 1:22). Elkanah bows to Hannah's wisdom and leaves with the rest of the family. And this year he not only will bring his yearly sacrifice to God but will make "his vow offering to the LORD" (verse 21 HCSB).

This "vow offering" may refer to a vow Elkanah had separately made to God, in the event his beloved Hannah give birth to a son. Or perhaps at some point during the year, Elkanah had learned about and then sanctioned the vow Hannah had already made to God. Such was the established practice of husbands who were responsible for their wives' actions.

Moses had told God's people, "When a man makes a vow to the LORD or swears an oath to put himself under an obligation, he must not break his word; he must do whatever he has promised" (Numbers 30:2 HCSB). On the other hand, if a woman made a vow and her husband heard about it but said nothing to her and didn't oppose her, then whatever vows she made were binding. But if he canceled her vows the day he heard about them, her vows were not binding. And because he canceled them, God absolved the woman of any responsibility. If a woman's husband didn't object to a vow she'd made when he heard about it and for days said nothing about it, then he was, in effect, confirming her vow (verses 10–15).

Vows to God were taken seriously. And sacrificial offerings were part of the bargain. Thus, it appears that the vow Hannah made to the Lord was not just backed up by but *approved* by Elkanah.

How wonderful when those we love the most support us in our heartfelt, selfless prayers, no matter how impossible or improbable our desires may seem. Elkanah's love for Hannah was truly bearing, believing, and hoping all things on her behalf. May we all experience such love.

> *Love bears all things, believes all things,*
> *hopes all things, endures all things.*
> 1 CORINTHIANS 13:7 ESV

Thank You, Lord, for the loved ones in my life who
support my dreams, desires, and prayers. Amen.

A Woman's Part

In Ramah Hannah sits alone,
To nurse and rear her infant son.
She will not go to worship there,
Till Samuel needs no more her care.
When weaned, she said, the work is mine,
To take him to the holy shrine.

The time had come for Elkanah's family to take the yearly trek to Shiloh to worship and sacrifice to the Lord. But Hannah and Samuel would be staying behind until the child was weaned (1 Samuel 1:22).

Hannah knew what the Lord had done for her. She knew that it was God who had formed her son's inward parts; that He had knit Samuel together in her womb; that He had intricately and wonderfully made her child. That was His part.

Hannah's part was to do what she had been built to do. To nurture her child. To make him as strong as she could by feeding him the milk from her breasts (1 Samuel 1:23), instead of hiring a wet nurse or using an animal's milk.

Perhaps because Hannah knew she would only have Samuel for a little while, maybe just three years, she looked at her role not so much as a duty but as a privilege. Also, for all she knew, this would be the only child she would ever be able to nurse and wean. And Hannah had to do so much more than wean Samuel off her breast milk. She had to care for him until he was strong enough to make the trip to Shiloh, old enough to learn from Eli how to care for the tabernacle and be useful to him.

Yet we still might wonder if Hannah was right to skip a worship event to take care of Samuel. Isn't God more important than any other being or obligation? Matthew Henry writes:

> *Hannah, though she felt a warm regard for the courts of God's house, begged to stay at home. God will have mercy, and not sacrifice. Those who are detained from public ordinances, by the nursing and tending of little children, may take comfort from this instance, and believe, that if they do that duty in a right spirit, God will graciously accept them therein.* *

Hannah shows us how God works in us to enable us "both to desire and to work out His good purpose" (Philippians 2:13 HCSB). Her story demonstrates that we have a partnership with God to do the best we can for Him and those He puts in our care.

Consider the ways in which you are partnering with God right now. How are you doing your part? How is God doing His?

We are His creation, created in Christ Jesus for good works, which God prepared ahead of time so that we should walk in them.
EPHESIANS 2:10 HCSB

Lord, give me the strength and wisdom to do my part.

* https://biblehub.com/commentaries/1_samuel/1-22.htm.

God's Word

Elkanah and his house approve,
And all is mutual peace and love.

Hannah told Elkanah she wouldn't be joining the rest of the family on the annual excursion to Shiloh, to worship and sacrifice to the Lord. Instead, she would be abstaining from such journeys until Samuel was weaned. Then she would "take him to the Tabernacle and leave him there with the LORD permanently" (1 Samuel 1:22 NLT).

To this, the loving and supportive Elkanah responded, "Do what seems best to you. Wait until you have weaned him; only may the LORD establish and confirm His word" (1 Samuel 1:23 AMP). The *Benson Commentary* explains Elkanah's words: "That is, may he perfect what he hath begun, by making the child grow up, and become fit for God's service, that he may be employed therein and accepted of God."*

God had planned perfectly for Samuel. He began by transforming Hannah's prayer into a reality. The persecuted yet persevering Hannah had gone to God, pleading for a miracle child, one she promised to raise as a Nazirite and then give back to God.

God had need of such a vessel as Hannah to bring His plan for Israel to fruition. He needed a high priest and a judge who would be loyal to Him alone. One who would dedicate his life to the service of the Lord. So God granted her selfless request. And now Elkanah, hearing the wisdom of Hannah's words about this precious child, was almost announcing a blessing over Samuel, that God not only would make this special child fit for God's service but also would use him to carry out His purposes.

God's Word tells us that His plans will succeed. That they are unstoppable. Job admitted this, saying to God, "I know that you can do all things, and that no purpose of yours can be thwarted" (Job 42:2 ESV). And God, speaking through Isaiah, said:

- "The Lord of Hosts has sworn: As I have purposed, so it will be; as I have planned it, so it will happen" (Isaiah 14:24 HCSB).

- "So will My word be which goes out of My mouth; it will not return to Me void (useless, without result), without accomplishing what I desire, and without succeeding in the matter for which I sent it" (Isaiah 55:11 AMP).

- "I am God, and no one is like Me. I declare the end from the beginning, and from long ago what is not yet done, saying: My plan will take place, and I will do all My will. . . . Yes, I have spoken; so I will also bring it about. I have planned it; I will also do it" (Isaiah 46:9–11 HCSB).

Believe God's promises. Take comfort that what He says He will do, He will do.

God, who began the good work within you, will continue his work until it is finally finished on the day when Christ Jesus returns.
PHILIPPIANS 1:6 NLT

Thank You, Lord, for being a promise keeper!

* https://biblehub.com/commentaries/1_samuel/1-23.htm.

Sacred Work

Oh sacred work! Oh sweet employ!
To rear for God that infant boy.
How pure the bliss the mother shares
With her first born a few short years.

What precious moments Hannah enjoyed with her newborn, moments she was engraving upon her mind and heart so that in the days after they parted, she would be able to recall his face, laugh, smile, and coos. Every time she looked at him, she was reminded of how he was her answer to prayer.

Yet Hannah also knew that, although she had gone through much labor to birth Samuel into the world, her work was not yet done. For she was now responsible for growing him into a child of God, preparing him for the work that lay ahead.

Hannah's responsibility to rear up her child to know, love, and worship God is an obligation every mother shares. And a duty God lays upon our hearts.

Moses told the Israelites to plant God's words in their hearts (Deuteronomy 6:6), saying, "Repeat them to your children. Talk about them when you sit in your house and when you walk along the road, when you lie down and when you get up" (verse 7 HCSB). Moses told the people God required them to fear Him, to love Him, to worship Him with all their heart and soul, and to walk in all His ways, keeping His commands and statutes (Deuteronomy 10:12–13). All for their own good.

Hannah was to teach these things to the young Samuel in three short years. And perhaps the best way she knew to do that was to

Holy Love

Infolding Samuel in her arms,
...d gazing on his youthful charms,
...: mother lifts her thoughts above,
And weaves a song of holy love.

...n Hannah's heart! As she held a cooing Samuel
...azing into his face, she was overcome by a wave
...l over her. She remembered the days before her
...uma and unhappiness that had assailed her, pre-
...king joy in the feast at Shiloh. And now here she
...ves on the answer to her prayers.

...ds us that when our hearts cannot help but sing,
...sing. When we are overflowing with joy, we must
...gs of holy love to the One who first loved us.

...last time you lifted your voice because you felt
...e love of God? When was the last time you sang
...who continually blesses you by providing you
..., shelter, love, purpose, and answers to prayer?
...n help us find the words to praise God for His
...to do is come up with a tune! Here are some
...trike a chord of praise within you!

...You, Lord, among the peoples; I will sing
...u among the nations. For Your faithful love is as
...eavens" (Psalm 57:9–10 HCSB).

set him an example. For because of his very young age, he might not fully know what her words meant. But he would remember how his mother often knelt to pray. He would remember the posture she took, the reverence she showed, the rhythm of her voice when she spoke to the Lord of Hosts.

Hannah taught Samuel the love and respect she had for God and His servants. With the neighbors and certainly other family members (e.g., Peninnah), Hannah taught Samuel patience and respect. She showed him how to take joy in simple things. Hannah may have taught him the whole of the Old Testament by teaching him the Golden Rule, which Jesus later worded so succinctly: "In everything treat others the same way you want them to treat you, for this is [the essence of] the Law and the [writings of the] Prophets" (Matthew 7:12 AMP).

Most importantly, Hannah taught Samuel to keep his word to God. And she did that by keeping her vow to give him, her answer to prayer, back into God's hands.

What are you teaching the children in your life?

> *Train up a child in the way he should go; even*
> *when he is old he will not depart from it.*
> PROVERBS 22:6 ESV

Lord, help me teach Your children by example.

Leaning into Love

What ties around her heart were spun,
By looks and smiles of her pure son:
Ties that her vow alone could sever,
That Samuel should be God's forever.

Hannah would only have her baby Samuel until he was weaned. Thus, in all probability, she must have spent every moment with him. These early ties she formed with Samuel in his first three years could never be broken. For just as he was the apple of her eye, she must have been the apple of his.

Recent studies have shown that intense closeness between mother and child is crucial for babies in the first three years. Apparently a mother's presence, emotionally and physically, from moment to moment, shields a child from stress. Thus, the more time a mom spends with her child, the less stressed and more nurtured the child becomes.

Yet how peaceful could these days Hannah spent with Samuel have been, with her knowing they would be over all too soon? It just may be that her faith was so pure, so tried-and-true, that she knew God would help her find a way through that eventual separation. Perhaps she so trusted God that what the future held was not her concern. Weaning Samuel was her responsibility, whereas planning her and Samuel's future was God's job.

Just as Hannah would never forget the child she nursed at her breast, she knew God would never forget her (Isaiah 49:15). Hannah was sure that whatever injury her parting from Samuel would cause, God would be there to pick up the pieces, to comfort her, to

shower her with love
answered her prayer
keep and provide for

Christian mother
only on loan from G
and taken away. Thu
years we have with t
adults. When they a
own way in the world
ance and affectionate

Just as Hannah
first three years of h
grieved by the realiz
God would have us le
while we can hold th
All the while knowin
give us all the comfo

As a mother

Lord, help m
You will

A
T

What joy was
in her arms,
of love that creste
child's birth, the tr
venting her from t
was, feasting her

Hannah remi
we are to let them
weave our own so

When was the
overwhelmed by t
praises to the On
with food, clothin

The psalms c
love. All we have
samples that may

- "I will prais
  praises to Y
  high as the

- "Your unfailing love is better than life itself; how I praise you!" (Psalm 63:3 NLT).

- "The LORD will send His faithful love by day; His song will be with me in the night—a prayer to the God of my life" (Psalm 42:8 HCSB).

- "I will sing of your strength; I will sing aloud of your stead-fast love in the morning. For you have been to me a fortress and a refuge in the day of my distress" (Psalm 59:16 ESV).

Psalm 59:16 truly might have resonated with Hannah, had the psalms been written during her life. For God surely was a fortress to her when she was in dire straits. Her reverent fear of God and her faithfulness to Him kept her from lashing back at Peninnah's cutting remarks. Hannah had held her tongue, shed wordless tears, and kept her eyes on and her hope in God. She had poured out her heart to the One who loves all and was rewarded for her patience, perseverance, and persistent faith in the One whose hands made the world.

Today, think of all the reasons you should be praising the God of love. Find a verse or two or three that will help you express that holy love. And you'll find yourself uplifted in both heart and song.

Give thanks to the LORD, for He is good. His love is eternal.
PSALM 136:1 HCSB

To You, Lord, I sing with joy!

In the Moment

"Sweet babe! I asked thee of the Lord,
And He has hearkened to my word;
A little season thou shalt rest
Upon thy mother's peaceful breast."

a mother often talks out loud, sharing her thoughts with the little one who lies upon her breast. Although she knows the child will not understand her words, still she says them, almost as if she were saying a prayer, comforting herself, reviewing in her own mind and heart what the future holds for them both.

You would think it a difficult thing for a mother to find herself growing so attached to a baby while knowing he would soon be out of her reach. Knowing that, once weaned, he would no longer be sleeping near her. There would be no checking in on him at night or during nap time, no tiptoeing into his room to make sure he was still breathing.

Yet this mother also knew the source of the blessing she had been given: the Lord. She knew her son was a direct answer to prayer. She knew that, in accordance with her vow, she would be giving him up, turning him over to God's care after just a brief season of bonding.

Just as Hannah knew from *whom* she'd received her blessing, the Giver knew the one to whom the blessing had been given. God knew that the selfless and humble Hannah would find peace no matter how little time she had her boy, that she would experience joy in the time she did have with him. For Hannah learned how to live in the moment. And she used those precious moments with Samuel wisely.

Instead of waking up and seeking worry, Hannah rose and sought God. She didn't fret about the day of parting that would eventually come, for she knew "each day has enough trouble of its own" (Matthew 6:34 AMP). In her wisdom, she was determined to "make the most of every opportunity" (Ephesians 5:16 NLT). Hannah knew a human's existence is "like the morning fog—it's here a little while, then it's gone" (James 4:14 NLT). So why would she waste time fretting over the future when she could look for and focus on peace and joy in the present moment?

How about you? Where do you stand on worries about the future? Do they overtake you, keep you from living in and finding peace in the present?

Perhaps it's time to ask the Lord to help you overcome endless and needless fretting. Ask Him to give you His peace, hope, and joy. God knows what you need, and He will provide it. Just be patient. He's got this. He's got you.

Let the peace of Christ [the inner calm of one who walks daily with Him] be the controlling factor in your hearts [deciding and settling questions that arise].
COLOSSIANS 3:15 AMP

Lord, give me the peace, hope, and joy that come with living in the present and leaving the future to You!

Gifting Back to God

"Dear as my soul thou art to me,
In thy bloom of infancy;
But thou art God's, and I resign
Thee wholly to the sacred shrine."

Hannah, in her desperation, in her offering to God of her very own self as vessel for His glory, had made a vow to the One who never changes. She had promised that if the Lord of Hosts gave her a son, she would return him to the Source who created all, to serve Him forevermore.

Hannah in her wisdom knew that "whatever we give to God, it is what we have first asked and received from him. All our gifts to him were first his gifts to us."*

This truth is rarely acknowledged or adhered to today. Too many people believe that all they have, all they have worked to earn—things tangible and intangible, both people and provisions— are their possessions entirely. Yet God makes it clear that *He* is the ultimate provider of our possessions and the supreme director of our lives.

During the Israelites' forty years in the wilderness, God had dwelled with them. And because of His presence, they had lacked nothing (Deuteronomy 2:7). For the Lord is the One who then and now supplies all needs (Philippians 4:19). And He never leaves His people "without evidence of himself and his goodness. For instance, he sends you rain and good crops and gives you food and joyful hearts" (Acts 14:17 NLT).

God alone is our Way Maker. He knows the best plan, has the

best ideas for our life. Each follower should be able to willingly admit to Him: "I know that the path of [life of] a man is not in himself; it is not within [the limited ability of] man [even one at his best] to choose and direct his steps [in life]" (Jeremiah 10:23 AMP).

Thus everything we have, all we possess, our entire life path, is in God's hands. To admit this brings us to act as Hannah did. As dear as some things and people in our lives are, they are really in God's hands, not our own. And in God's hands is exactly where we should place them. After all, the Great Provider is also the Great Protector. We can trust Him to guide us, for He can see the beginning, middle, and end of all our stories.

So today, take your cue from Hannah. Gift all you are and hope to be, all you have and hope to have to God. Surrender your life, your world, your beginning, middle, and end to God. And you will be filled to overflowing with His provision and joy.

The earth and everything in it, the world and
its inhabitants, belong to the LORD.
PSALM 24:1 HCSB

Lord, I gift back to You all I am, all I have, and all I hope to be.

* *Matthew Henry's Concise Commentary*, https://biblehub.com/commentaries/1_samuel/1-23.htm.

Finding a Reward

"Thy mother has her pure reward
In lending thee unto the Lord.
In Shiloh we will often meet,
And worship at the mercy seat."

Hannah was willing to sacrifice to God the greatest thing in her possession: her firstborn and, so far, only son. God had kept His end of the bargain and it would soon be time for her to keep hers. The consolation she had in this endeavor was threefold: First, she was lending her son to the Lord, the best and most loving Master a young man could desire. Second, she would still be able to visit her son whenever she and Elkanah traveled to Shiloh to worship the Lord. And third, she resolved to find joy in the now by spending precious quality time with Samuel.

Hannah was, in a sense, preparing herself for the situation that was to come, the day she would leave Samuel at the tabernacle in Shiloh where he would be trained by the priests to serve the Lord. In the most difficult circumstances a mother could conceive, Hannah began to employ the ideas that would later be recorded in 1 Thessalonians 5:16–19.

By looking to God and her faith, Hannah found a way to rejoice. Each thought, each statement she spoke was like a prayer. She could, in her gratefulness to God, imagine that she would be rewarded for lending Samuel back to Him. For her desires and will were aligned with God's, and she refused to squelch the Spirit He had planted within her, the One who gave her the courage, strength, and love she needed to walk in the path God had laid out for her.

Every Christian can follow Hannah's path. Every woman can find God's reward in her circumstances, in her path, in her heart, if she would just do as Hannah did.

It may not be easy at first to find a way to rejoice in the direst of circumstances. Perhaps start out with smaller setbacks, looking for reasons to give God thanks, and work your way up to those larger difficulties that might prove more difficult. Instead of getting upset over what didn't go your way, rejoice! Thank God for giving you the opportunity to experience what has happened. That can be your lead-in to prayer, as you proceed to take all your concerns to Him.

Whatever you do, make sure you don't strangle the Spirit God has planted within you. Do not "[subdue, or be unresponsive to the working and guidance of] the [Holy] Spirit" (1 Thessalonians 5:19 AMP). Instead, keep yourself clued in to Him at every moment. And then you too will find your joyous reward no matter what you face.

Rejoice always, pray without ceasing, give thanks in all circumstances; for this is the will of God in Christ Jesus for you. Do not quench the Spirit.
1 THESSALONIANS 5:16–19 ESV

Lord, help me rejoice no matter how dark my clouds!

Together Forever

"And when thy mother's race is run,
And all thy works of love are done;
When toils are ended, partings o'er;
Will rest in God forevermore."

Knowing she would soon have to part with her son to make good on her vow, Hannah ruminated on an eternal consolation: although she and Samuel might not see much of each other in their present life, they would eventually be reunited in the afterlife.

The Old Testament contains hints that Jews believed in an afterlife. The first is found in Genesis 25:8 (AMP): "Abraham breathed his last and he died at a good old age, an old man who was satisfied [with life]; and he was gathered to his people [who had preceded him in death]."

In 2 Samuel, the prophet Nathan confronted King David about his adultery with Bathsheba and his scheming to have Bathsheba's husband, Uriah, die in battle, clearing the path for David to take Bathsheba as his own wife. After David admitted having sinned against God in both cases, Nathan told him: "The LORD has taken away your sin; you will not die. However, because you treated the LORD with such contempt in this matter, the son born to you will die" (2 Samuel 12:13–14 HCSB).

After Nathan left, David's son from Bathsheba grew ill. Despite David's pleading with God, fasting and lying prostrate on the ground, his son died within the week. David then rose, washed, dressed, and worshipped the Lord. Once back home, David asked for food. For he said, "While the baby was alive, I fasted and wept because I thought, 'Who knows? The LORD may be gracious to me and let him live.' But now that he is dead, why should I fast? Can I bring him back again? I'll go to him, but he will never return to me" (2 Samuel 12:22–23 HCSB).

Fortunately, when Jesus came, He didn't *hint* at an afterlife. He described it!

> *"Don't let your hearts be troubled. Trust in God, and trust also in me. There is more than enough room in my Father's home. If this were not so, would I have told you that I am going to prepare a place for you? When everything is ready, I will come and get you, so that you will always be with me where I am." (John 14:1–3 NLT)*

Then, while Jesus was still on earth, He met with two amazing, but already dead, men of God in front of His own disciples. Those men were Moses and Elijah! The disciples who witnessed the transformational encounter were Peter, James, and John.

All believers can be reassured that those they have to part with in this life they will see again in the afterlife, if those loved ones have trusted in Jesus as their Savior. Praise God!

> *If I ascend to heaven, you are there!*
> PSALM 139:8 ESV

> *Lord, thank You for allowing me to live with You and my believing loved ones forever!*

Keeping Vows

The mother keeps her solemn vow,
And weans her first born son, and now
She leads him to the holy shrine,
With year old bullocks, flour, and wine.

Samuel has been weaned. And the time Hannah selected to take him to the Lord, to serve at His house forever in keeping with her vow, has arrived.

We can imagine how Hannah prepared herself and Samuel for the journey to Shiloh. She most likely carefully packed the little robe she had lovingly made for him, the one he would wear as he served in the tabernacle of the Lord. She may then have dressed him in a more durable outfit for the journey itself.

Before and during the journey, we can imagine the silent support Elkanah gave to the wife he loved best, knowing how difficult it would be for her to take her son to the tabernacle for the first time, only to leave him there and then take the long trek back home where things would, without the young Samuel there, be quiet and a bit lonely for both of them.

On that journey to Shiloh, we may wonder how much Hannah may have wanted to hold her child, yet restrained herself from doing so, instead keeping her distance a bit so as not to make the final parting even harder for her and the boy.

Yet we know enough of Hannah's character, her faithfulness to the Lord, to know she would ultimately keep her vow. That she would return to God's hands the child who was already His, the gift He had originally given her that she was now giving back.

The wonder of it all is that even the bull, flour, and wine that Elkanah brought with his family, as well as the son, were offerings that God didn't need, per se. He clearly told His faithful people in Psalm 50: "I have no complaint about your sacrifices or the burnt offerings you constantly offer. But I do not need the bulls from your barns or the goats from your pens. For all the animals of the forest are mine, and I own the cattle on a thousand hills" (verses 8–10 NLT).

What God truly wants from you, His faithful follower, is for you to "make thankfulness your sacrifice to God, and keep the vows you made to the Most High. Then call on me when you are in trouble, and I will rescue you, and you will give me glory" (Psalm 50:14–15 NLT).

God would have us realize that it's not so much a sacrifice He wants or needs, but rather a heart dedicated to Him, loyal to Him, ready to give all to Him.

And in keeping her vow, in turning over her son, Hannah did just that. She gave God her all.

Giving thanks is a sacrifice that truly honors me.
PSALM 50:23 NLT

Lord, I give to You all I am and hope to be.

Total Trust

They eat yet not the sacred feast.
Before the robed and mitered priest
Elkanah and the mother stand,
With little Samuel in her hand.

The last time Hannah had been to Shiloh, she had been so distraught that she could neither eat nor stop crying. Because of her distress at being harassed and tortured by Peninnah's words and behavior, Hannah had risen from their sacrificial feast and made her way to the tent of meeting.

When down on her knees, pleading with God, Hannah had surrendered herself to God. Her mind, body, heart, soul, and spirit were His. And in that surrendering, she found God answering her deepest need and desire.

Now Hannah was before God once more with her answer to prayer in hand. And once more she was going to surrender the most precious part of herself—her first and only son, Samuel—to God's care. No strings attached. No bargains made. Before the altar, Hannah brought Samuel to the One she trusted most.

In this, Hannah was like Abraham. The man who had only one son through his wife Sarah. The one they named Isaac. He too brought his son to God. He surrendered his pride and joy to the Master Creator and Keeper of Promises. Just as Abraham was about to slay the sacrifice God required of him, his precious son, God stayed his hand. The Angel of the Lord said to him, "Don't lay a hand on the boy! . . . Do not hurt him in any way, for now I know that you truly fear God. You have not withheld from me even your son, your only son" (Genesis 22:12 NLT). Then Abraham looked up and saw a ram caught in a thicket. And so he offered that in place of his son.

We might ask, how could a parent do such a thing? Maybe a father could, but could a mother, one who had labored for and birthed the child? Abraham could do it because he believed in God's promises. He believed in God's power. "Abraham reasoned that if Isaac died, God was able to bring him back to life again. And in a sense, Abraham did receive his son back from the dead" (Hebrews 11:19 NLT).

Just as Abraham believed in and trusted in God, Hannah believed in and trusted in God. Although she didn't know exactly what it would mean for Samuel to serve God, she freely surrendered him to God's loving care. No prayer of "Here he is, Lord. Please don't let anything happen to him." No second-guessing of her vow. Just a willing surrender.

May we all surrender to God our most precious answers to prayer. And trust Him with their lives and futures.

> *Those who know your name trust in you, for you,*
> *O Lord, do not abandon those who search for you.*
> PSALM 9:10 NLT

To You, God, I surrender all. In You I trust.

Faint or Fervent?

And said: "I am that sorrowing one
Thy watchful eyes once gazed upon,
And saw imploring God to hear
Her wrestling, agonizing prayer."

Seeing Eli the priest, Hannah reminds him of who she is, saying, "Oh, my lord! As [surely as] your soul lives, my lord, I am the woman who stood beside you here, praying to the LORD" (1 Samuel 1:26 AMP).

Yet having witnessed that scene through the words of scripture, we know that what the barren Hannah had been doing was not merely praying. Having come to the end of herself, she was weeping out of agony and desperation. And amid those tears, she made a vow to God part of her petition to Him, demonstrating her commitment to and expectation of seeing her prayer answered by the all-powerful Lord of Hosts.

In this way, Hannah demonstrated what it means to wrestle in prayer. Her request, although wordless, was no calm approach. No flowery words were said. This was a woman getting down on her knees and pouring out her soul to the Lord.

If Hannah could have described her wrestling in prayer at the altar in Shiloh, she may have found the words of Psalm 77 very fitting: "In the day of my trouble I seek the Lord; in the night my hand is stretched out without wearying; my soul refuses to be comforted. When I remember God, I moan; when I meditate, my spirit faints. . . . You hold my eyelids open; I am so troubled that I cannot speak" (verses 2–4 ESV).

Let us pause and consider our own prayers, ones that may have gone unanswered. Have we, like Hannah, gone to God and poured out our hearts to Him with sincere tears and cries of agony? Or are our prayers dull, rambling, aimless, and disjointed?

What about our prayers for other people? Are they also weak and meandering? Are we faint or fervent in our intercessory prayers?

And what about our sense of expectation? Do we confidently believe God will answer our prayers? Or do we feel as if our words are going nowhere, that we're just putting our prayers out there so we can tick "prayer time" off our ever-expanding to-do list?

And what about our persistence in prayer? Do we ask once and figure we're done? Or do we go before God with our requests continually, asking Him, each time we approach His throne, to shape our petitions so they line up with His will?

Hannah is our example of what a fervent petitioner should look like. She shows us how to pour our all into our prayers. How to be specific in our requests, to have a sense of expectation, and to be persistent in approaching the throne of grace.

All these with one accord were devoting themselves to prayer.
Acts 1:14 esv

Lord, please help me to be devoted and fervent in prayer.

Dedicated to God

"For this dear child I prayed, and He
Has heard my cry of agony;
And now I lend him to the Giver,
To serve Him in His courts forever."

H annah goes further into her explanation to Eli the priest, wanting him to know exactly who she is. So she says to him, "For this child I prayed, and the Lord has granted me my request which I asked of Him. Therefore I have also dedicated him to the Lord; as long as he lives he is dedicated to the Lord" (1 Samuel 1:27–28 AMP).

You can almost hear the excitement in Hannah's voice. She is showing the proof of her answered prayer to Eli. "Look here! This is the answer to my prayer, in the flesh! God gave him to me, and now I'm dedicating him to God for the rest of his life—just as I promised!

"You must remember me! After I told you about how I was not drunk with wine but was pouring out my heart to God, 'praying from the depth of my anguish and resentment' (1 Samuel 1:16 HCSB), you said—I'll never forget your exact words—you said, 'Leave in peace, and may God give you what you have asked for'!

"Anyway, here he is"—putting Samuel's hand in Eli's—"ready and willing and able to serve you in God's work."

Hannah gives her son to Eli with no apparent hesitation. Her doing so reminds us of how important it is that God's people are strong in their spirituality, firm in their faith, confident in their commitment to Him.

For had Hannah been weak and yielding in her spirituality and faith, had she been fearful, doubtful, or unsure in her commitment to God, she wouldn't have made good on her vow to the Lord. Samuel never would have been given back to God, put in His care. And if Samuel had remained with his mom, the nation of Israel may have fallen further into rack and ruin. God then may have looked down at humankind "to see if there is one who is wise, one who seeks God" and concluded that "all have turned away; all alike have become corrupt. There is no one who does good, not even one" (Psalm 53:2–3 HCSB). But thank God, Hannah stayed true to her word and to God, as He asks us all to do.

God is still looking for women, with or without children, who are strong in their spirituality. Women who are firm in their faith. Women who are confidently committed to serving God, doing His will, walking His way. His hope lies in Hannahs. Will you be one?

Brothers and sisters, be strong and immovable. Always
work enthusiastically for the Lord, for you know that
nothing you do for the Lord is ever useless.
1 CORINTHIANS 15:58 NLT

Lord, help me be strong in spirit, firm in faith,
and confident in my commitment to You.

From Pain to Prayer to Patience to Praise

As one inspired the mother stands,
With eyes upraised, and lifted hands.

After Hannah turned her first and only son, Samuel, over to Eli the high priest, scripture tells us, "They worshiped the LORD there" (1 Samuel 1:28 AMP). There were no anguished cries of grief that the boy Samuel would no longer reside with his family but in God's house. There were no regrets that this precious, prayed-for child would be far from his mother's reach from now on. There was only praise.

Hannah's journey had begun amid the pain of being barren, and then being taunted and mistreated because of that barrenness. It was that pain that brought her to the house of God, where she threw herself down and poured herself out in prayer. And there before His throne, Hannah took a leap of faith, vowing that if God would give her a son, she would give him back to God for His service.

Hannah then went home and waited patiently until she conceived, labored, and birthed a son. And to this son she imparted all her wisdom from and knowledge of God. She was an example to him of commitment to the Holy One.

When the boy was ready, in accordance with her vow to God, she brought him back to God's house and turned the gift over to the Giver. She worshipped the Lord there, bursting into praise, "with eyes upraised, and lifted hands."

We know Hannah's actions, her example of making good on her

word to the Lord, made an impression on her son. For in 1 Samuel 15:22 (NLT), we read of him saying, "What is more pleasing to the LORD: your burnt offerings and sacrifices or your obedience to his voice? Listen! Obedience is better than sacrifice, and submission is better than offering the fat of rams."

What Hannah did was a sacrifice on her part. But because she was so faithful to God, she was able to go right from sacrifice to praise, showing that she wasn't just looking out for herself but was concerned with what she could do for God, for her nation of Israel, for her faith (Philippians 2:4). Her pivoting immediately from sacrifice to praise proved she loved God more than her son (Matthew 10:37).

The sacrifice Hannah made is one God would encourage all His followers to make. We're to continually offer up to Him our sacrifice of praise. At the same time, we're not to stop doing good but to continue sharing what we have for the benefit and good of all, "for such sacrifices are pleasing to God" (Hebrews 13:15–16 ESV).

May we follow Hannah's selfless and faithful pattern, moving from our pain to prayer to patience to praise, giving thanks to God through it all.

> *You who stand in the house of the LORD. . .praise the LORD.*
> PSALM 135:2–3 AMP

To You, Lord, I lift my praise!

A Song to God

And 'mid the gathered, waiting throng,
She pours her soul to God in song.

*a*t the beginning of 1 Samuel 2, we find Hannah bursting out in song. Instead of being utterly cast down because she will be leaving her beloved son, Samuel, behind, she is looking up, moving forward, praising God for what He has done and what He will do for her and her people.

In the next ten verses, Hannah uses prayer, poetry, and prophecy in a song of praise to God, taking her place among the ranks of singers such as Miriam, Deborah, Elizabeth, Zechariah, David, and other psalmists and prophets. She has moved from desperate prayer into distinct praise, filled with thanksgiving for what God has done in her life. Hannah has followed the suggestions penned by James in his New Testament letter to the scattered Hebrew tribes: "Is anyone among you suffering? He must pray. Is anyone joyful? He is to sing praises [to God]" (James 5:13 AMP).

Hannah's prayer-song asks for nothing from the Lord. Instead, she thanks Him for what He has done in the past, then flows into the confidence she has in the future. She who, in her despair, had fled to and fallen on her knees before and poured out her heart to the Rock of Israel now, in her triumph, pours out her soul to God with a joyful song of thanksgiving.

Ellicott's Commentary for English Readers says:

> *These true, beautiful thoughts the Spirit of the Lord*
> *first planted in Hannah's heart, and then gave her*

lips, grace and power to utter them in the sublime
language of her hymn, which became one of the
loved songs of the people, and as such was handed
down from father to son [and from mother to
daughter], from generation to generation, in Israel,
in the very words which first fell from the blessed
mother of the child-prophet in her quiet home of
"Ramah of the Watchers."*

Two songs in the Bible are comparable to Hannah's: the song of David in 2 Samuel 22 and the Magnificat of Mary in Luke 1:46–55. These three reveal how God freely gives His grace to the unworthy, how He defeats the enemy, and how He can turn worldly events upside down to achieve His purposes.

Chances are you have been on bended knee before the Rock of Ages and poured out your heart. Perhaps you too cried as if the world was against you, as if your dreams would never bear fruit. Maybe the Lord even answered your prayer in a way that was beyond imagining. Perhaps today you would like to gift the God of answered prayer with your own joyful song of thanksgiving.

Sing to Him a new song.
PSALM 33:3 AMP

To You I come, Rock of Ages, singing my praise and thanks.

* https://biblehub.com/commentaries/1_samuel/2-1.htm.

Righteous Rejoicing

My soul rejoiceth in the Lord,
From whom my comfort flows.

When the barren and bruised Hannah ran to the Lord, His presence alone was where she found comfort. There alone she willingly offered herself up to be used as a vessel for God, asking once more to be gifted with a child she would then return to Him. So it seems only right that, having had her prayer answered, she should now stand up in public in that place and sing at the top of her voice, "My heart rejoices in the LORD" (1 Samuel 2:1 HCSB).

The virgin Mary's song echoes Hannah's. For this young girl, who was right with God, had been told by the angel Gabriel that she, a virgin, would give birth to Jesus. That the Holy Spirit would come upon her and the power of the Most High would overshadow her. That the One conceived within her would "be called the Son of the Most High" (Luke 1:32 HCSB). As alarming as this news may have sounded to a young girl's ears, Mary acquiesced to God's plan, allowing Him to use her as His vessel.

When Mary later visited her elderly cousin Elizabeth, miraculously pregnant in her old age, the child within Elizabeth leaped in her womb, prompting her to call Mary "the mother of my Lord" (Luke 1:43 HCSB). Hearing this greeting, Mary began her own song, saying, "My soul proclaims the greatness of the Lord, and my spirit has rejoiced in God my Savior" (verses 46–47 HCSB).

Here we have three women who are right with the Lord and cannot help but burst out in a song of praise. And it is to them the writer of Psalm 33 speaks, saying, "Rejoice in the LORD, you righteous ones; praise is becoming and appropriate for those who are upright [in heart—those with moral integrity and godly character]" (verse 1 AMP).

Two of these three women, namely Hannah and Elizabeth, had been transformed from barren to fruitful. Mary, a virgin, had not been barren but had yet to be intimate with a man. And she too soon found herself pregnant. For Mary, who believed that nothing would be impossible for God (Luke 1:37–38), that the word He had spoken to her through Gabriel would be fulfilled (verse 45), had also undergone a dramatic transformation.

When God works within us, seeks to use us as His vessels, transforming us in a way we had never dreamed or imagined so that His plan for this world can be advanced, we too should be rejoicing. Not just with friends, family, and neighbors, but with God. The One we trust to answer our prayers and care for us.

> *In Him our heart rejoices, because we trust [lean on,*
> *rely on, and are confident] in His holy name.*
> PSALM 33:21 AMP

In You, Lord, my heart rejoices! To You my spirit sings!

Strength and Salvation

Exalted is my horn in God
O'er all my subtle foes.

In 1 Samuel 2:1 (AMP), Hannah sings, "My horn (strength) is lifted up in the LORD, my mouth has opened wide [to speak boldly] against my enemies, because I rejoice in Your salvation." In these words, she gives us a taste of the strength she found in God.

Horns of animals represented their strength, symbolizing the power the animal had in lifting its horn-adorned head high with pride. It was just this type of strength Hannah gained from God, not only from His presence but from His answer to prayer (Samuel). Now, with her son in her arms and later by her side, she could speak boldly to those who treated her cruelly (namely, Peninnah) when she had been barren.

Hannah also could rejoice at how God had saved her from a life of barrenness. Mary echoes these sentiments, singing, "And my spirit has rejoiced in God my Savior" (Luke 1:47 AMP).

This same strength and salvation appears in other places in scripture:

- "The LORD is my light and my *salvation*—whom should I fear? The LORD is the *stronghold* of my life—of whom should I be afraid?" (Psalm 27:1 HCSB, emphasis added).

- "The *salvation* of the righteous is from the LORD; he is their *stronghold* in the time of trouble" (Psalm 37:39 ESV, emphasis added).

- "He alone is my rock and my *salvation*, my *stronghold*; I will never be shaken" (Psalm 62:2 HCSB, emphasis added).

- "God is my *salvation*; I will trust Him and not be afraid, for Yah, the LORD, is my *strength* and my song" (Isaiah 12:2 HCSB, emphasis added).

- "The LORD your God is in your midst, a *mighty* one who will *save*" (Zephaniah 3:17 ESV, emphasis added).

God's strength and His ability to save you are inextricably linked. One cannot and does not come without the other. That is what Hannah, feeling empty, fruitless, and weary, discovered when she went to God and poured out all her angst. In return, God gave her the strength to stand. He saved her from the abuse of others. At the same time, He used her to birth a boy who would grow up to become a priest and judge who would one day save His people Israel.

When you feel empty, fruitless, and weary, go to God. Kneel before Him. Pour out all the angst and grief within you. Allow your tears to dampen His breast. Present your petition. Then rise, knowing, never doubting, that He has the strength and the power to do the impossible. To make all His promises to you come to fruition. To lift you up so that you too can boldly stand against those who have scorned and abused you.

> *"The LORD is my strength and my song,*
> *and he has become my salvation."*
> EXODUS 15:2 ESV

Lift me, Lord, with Your strength and saving power.

Holiness

Pure holiness is Thine, O Lord!
Unshaken is Thy throne.

Having lifted some personal exultations to God in verse 1, Hannah now begins to praise God in general, singing, "There is no one holy like the Lord" (1 Samuel 2:2 HCSB, echoed by Mary in Luke 1:49).

This God, our God, is unique. No one else is purely holy like Him. He is holiness personified. *Gill's Exposition of the Entire Bible* helps us understand this facet of God, explaining:

> *In all his ways and works; [God] is essentially, originally, independently, perfectly, and immutably holy, as others are not. Angels are holy, but not of themselves; their holiness is from the Lord. . . . Though there is a likeness of the holiness of God in [men], being made partakers of the divine nature; it is far from an equality to it; for the holiness of the best of men is imperfect.**

It was this holy God who acted on Hannah's behalf, responding to her righteousness, her willingness, her selflessness by pouring His love and grace upon her. By answering her prayer, He not only rid her of those abusing her but used her to raise up a man who would lead Israel out of the darkness and into His light.

Yet a holy God can only do such things through people who trust in Him. People who stay true to their word—as well as His. People who endeavor to be holy as He is holy.

The writer of Hebrews encourages us to "strive for peace with everyone, and for the holiness without which no one will see the Lord" (12:14 ESV). In fact, God's ultimate desire is for us to be holy: "God's will is for you to be holy" (1 Thessalonians 4:3 NLT), a position made attainable to us because "God made Christ, who never sinned, to be the offering for our sin, so that we could be made right with God through Christ" (2 Corinthians 5:21 NLT).

Yet to become holy is difficult at best. There is no way we can do such work on our own. Thankfully, Paul gives us some guidance in this regard: "Work out your salvation. . .with awe-inspired fear and trembling. . . . For it is [not your strength, but it is] God who is effectively at work in you, both to will and to work [that is, strengthening, energizing, and creating in you the longing and the ability to fulfill your purpose] for His good pleasure" (Philippians 2:12–13 AMP).

If you haven't already, allow God to work within you to make you holy. Then you too can be used by Him to further His kingdom.

*If anyone cleanses himself from what is dishonorable,
he will be a vessel for honorable use, set apart as
holy, useful. . .ready for every good work.*
2 TIMOTHY 2:21 ESV

---

*I present myself to You in this moment, Lord.
Make me holy, set apart for Your use.*

* https://biblehub.com/commentaries/1_samuel/2-2.htm.

The Everlasting Rock

Thou art the everlasting Rock,
And Thou art God alone.

Hannah had been walking on shifting sands. Each time Peninnah would make a nasty remark about Hannah's barrenness, the force of it would cause Hannah to lose not just her appetite and happiness but her balance and footing.

All that changed after Hannah spent time at the tabernacle in Shiloh. For there, on her knees before the Rock of Ages, she made a vow for a son. One that was then underlined by Eli the high priest, who told her, "Go in peace, and may the God of Israel grant the petition you've requested from Him" (1 Samuel 1:17 HCSB). His words gave her the hope and confidence that her request would indeed be granted. She had finally found solid ground on which to stand. And now that her answer to prayer had been delivered and her vow fulfilled, Hannah sang out, "There is no one besides You, there is no Rock like our God" (2:2 AMP).

Likening God to a rock was a well-known simile among the people of Israel. There is no better word to describe God's permanence, solidity, prominence, protection, security, unchangeableness, and majesty in the minds of those who wandered in the desert wilderness.

About God, Moses sang, "He is the Rock; his deeds are perfect" (Deuteronomy 32:4 NLT). God Himself said, through Isaiah, "You are My witnesses. Is there any God besides Me, or is there any other Rock? I know of none" (Isaiah 44:8 NASB). David wrote, "Blessed be the LORD, my rock, who trains my hands for war, and my fingers for battle" (Psalm 144:1 NASB); as well as, "In You, LORD, I have taken refuge. . . . Incline Your ear to me, rescue me quickly; be a rock of strength for me, a stronghold to save me. For You are my rock and my fortress; for the sake of Your name You will lead me and guide me" (Psalm 31:1–3 NASB).

Jesus Himself is referred to as a rock in Romans 9:33 (NASB): "Just as it is written, 'Behold, I am laying in Zion a stone of stumbling and a rock of offense, and the one who believes in Him will not be put to shame.'" In 1 Corinthians 10:4 (NASB), Paul talks about the wandering Israelites, writing, "All drank the same spiritual drink, for they were drinking from a spiritual rock which followed them; and the rock was Christ."

When you are being buffeted by the enemy, losing your foothold, and need something firm to stand on, go to God, your Rock. In His presence, you'll find all the peace and stability you need to stand firm.

You will keep the mind that is dependent on You in perfect
peace, for it is trusting in You. Trust in the LORD forever,
because in Yah, the LORD, is an everlasting rock!
ISAIAH 26:3–4 HCSB

Rock of Ages, help me find the solid
ground I need to stand firm in You!

Pride Fall

Talk not in pride and arrogance,
Ye mortals weak and frail.

Following on the heels of Hannah's proclamation that God is her Rock, she sings out a warning: "Do not go on boasting so very proudly, do not let arrogance come out of your mouth" (1 Samuel 2:3 AMP). Most Bible scholars think she was referring to the one who had, in her arrogance, bad-mouthed Hannah because of her barrenness. And that woman was Peninnah, the mother of many (verse 5).

Peninnah was earlier referred to as "Hannah's rival" who "provoked her bitterly, to irritate and embarrass her, because the LORD had left her childless. So it happened year after year, whenever she went up to the house of the LORD, Peninnah provoked her; so she wept and would not eat" (1 Samuel 1:6–7 AMP).

If Hannah did indeed intend these lines of her song for Peninnah, not mentioning her rival by name speaks of Hannah's discretion. Even though this woman had caused Hannah much sorrow, she would not reveal her name and thus saved her from the condemnation of others.

In His Word, God makes it clear how much He detests people who harbor and display pride and arrogance. In fact, pride is one of the first things mentioned in the list of "six things the LORD hates; indeed, seven are repulsive to Him: a proud look [the attitude that makes one overestimate oneself and discount others]. . ." (Proverbs 6:16–17 AMP).

Chances are you know people who display both pride and arrogance. You may even have been the target of their gibes and barbs.

You may have suffered the same kind of pain Hannah experienced at the hands of Peninnah. And so you might understand why God hates pride and arrogance so much. Enough so that you must hate whatever pride and arrogance you yourself may harbor.

Perhaps deep within, you hold yourself above others. Yet you say nothing aloud. If this is the case, make it your aim to pray that haughtiness out of yourself. Ask God for help, for as the psalmist writes, although "the LORD protects those who are loyal to him. . .he harshly punishes the arrogant" (Psalm 31:23 NLT).

Perhaps you are free from being prideful and arrogant, yet you're surrounded by those who are. Paul, in his second letter to Timothy, expects their population to be plentiful in the last days, writing:

> *For people will be lovers of self, lovers of money, boastful, proud, blasphemers, disobedient to parents, ungrateful, unholy, unloving, irreconcilable, slanderers, without self-control, brutal, without love for what is good, traitors, reckless, conceited, lovers of pleasure rather than lovers of God, holding to the form of godliness but denying its power.*
> *(2 Timothy 3:2–5 HCSB)*

The solution? "Avoid these people!" (verse 5 HCSB). And remember:

> *Pride goes before destruction, and haughtiness before a fall.*
> PROVERBS 16:18 NLT

Help me, Lord, to be humble in both Your eyes and mine.

Weighing In

The Lord beholds the deeds of men,
And weighs them in his scale.

Following Hannah's remark about the debasing words of others is her next line, "For the LORD is a God of knowledge, and by Him actions are weighed (examined)" (1 Samuel 2:3 AMP). This may imply that although Hannah did not include Peninnah's name when she sang of the arrogant and prideful words of others, *God* knows what each person thinks, does, and says. And God will hold each person (including Peninnah) accountable for it.

Understanding that God knows what each of us does and that one day He will weigh and examine our actions should make us pause. At the same time, we must realize that God knows each one of us inside and out. As David wrote, "LORD, You have searched me and known me. You know when I sit down and when I stand up; You understand my thoughts from far away. You observe my travels and my rest; You are aware of all my ways. Before a word is on my tongue, You know all about it, LORD" (Psalm 139:1–4 HCSB).

That God knows what we're thinking and doing, as well as our intents, is made very clear by the story of Ananias and Sapphira. This couple had sold a piece of land and decided to give the proceeds to the group of believers who were sharing everything. But the couple held back part of the proceeds. When Ananias laid the money at Peter's feet, Peter asked, "Ananias, why has Satan filled your heart to lie to the Holy Spirit and keep back part of the proceeds from the field? . . . You have not lied to men but to God!" (Acts 5:3–4 HCSB). Ananias dropped dead on the spot. Later on that same day, his wife dropped dead too.

Knowing God can read your mind and your heart may sound scary to some. Yet within this knowledge lies hope. For God provides us a way to rein in our thoughts, allowing us to think carefully before we act!

We can come before God the first thing each day and ask Him to help us with our hearts, praying, "Search me, O God, and know my heart; test me and know my anxious thoughts. Point out anything in me that offends you, and lead me along the path of everlasting life" (Psalm 139:23–24 NLT). We can present our bodies to Him "as a living sacrifice, holy and acceptable" (Romans 12:1 ESV). We can make sure we are not conformed to this world but transformed by renewing our minds so that we "may discern what is the good, pleasing, and perfect will of God" (Romans 12:2 HCSB). And, most important of all, we can. . .

Take every thought captive to obey Christ.
2 CORINTHIANS 10:5 ESV

Lord, here I am. Search my heart. Renew my mind so that all I think and do will please You. In Jesus' name, amen.

The Almighty

The boasting, mighty warrior's bow
Is broken in his hand. . . .

In 1 Samuel 2:4 (AMP), Hannah sings of how "the bows of the mighty are broken" by the Lord. Time and time again God provides evidence for this statement.

We see the most notable demonstration of God breaking the power of the mighty in Exodus 14. There God showed His tremendous power by telling Moses to position His people, who had just left Egypt, between the wilderness and the sea. He wanted Pharaoh to think the Israelites were "wandering around the land in confusion; the wilderness [having] boxed them in" (Exodus 14:3 HCSB). God's next move was to harden Pharaoh's heart again so that he would go after God's people. In saving them, God would then receive all the glory, making sure all would know He is Yahweh.

So the Israelites camped by the sea. And when Pharaoh got wind of it, he, with his newly hardened heart, had a change of mind and went after God's people. "So he got his chariot ready and took his troops with him; he took 600 of the best chariots and all the rest of the chariots of Egypt, with officers in each one" (Exodus 14:6–7 HCSB).

When the Israelites saw that huge army coming at them, they cried out to the Lord for help and then blamed Moses, asking him why he had put them in this position. They began complaining that they would have been better off if they'd just stayed in Egypt. There they would still be enslaved and unhappy but alive.

That's when Moses shared some wonderfully encouraging words with them: "Don't be afraid. Stand firm and see the LORD's salvation He will provide for you today; for the Egyptians you see today, you will never see again. The LORD will fight for you" (Exodus 14:13–14 HCSB).

Then God told Moses to tell the Israelites to break camp. To allow them to walk through the sea on dry ground, Moses would simply lift up his staff, stretch it out over the sea, and in so doing part the waters.

God's plan was to keep the seabed exposed only as the Israelites crossed over. Then, when Pharaoh and his army of chariots pursued them, their wheels would get stuck, the Egyptians would panic, and Moses would stretch out his hand to bring the waters back, drowning the lot of them. In the end, not one of the Egyptians would be left alive—but God's people would be safe on the other side.

When you feel as if you have no strength or power, remember who is on your side: the One who can break the power of the mighty.

He who dwells in the shelter of the Most High will
remain secure and rest in the shadow of the Almighty
[whose power no enemy can withstand].
PSALM 91:1 AMP

With You in my life, Lord, I have nothing to fear.

Clothed with Strength

. . .While wavering hosts, renewed in strength,
With noble vigor stand.

In the next verse of Hannah's song, she makes clear that as "the bows of the warriors are broken" by God, "the feeble are clothed with strength" (1 Samuel 2:4 HCSB). And once again, scripture shows us examples of this, the most notable being Gideon.

During the days of the judges, "the people of Israel did what was evil in the sight of the LORD, and the LORD gave them into the hand of Midian seven years" (Judges 6:1 ESV). Because the Midianites kept raiding Israel, destroying their crops and livestock, the Israelites cried out to God for help. That's when the Angel of the Lord visited Gideon, who was hiding out in a winepress where he was threshing wheat out of sight of the Midianites.

The Angel of the Lord told Gideon, "The LORD is with you, O mighty man of valor" (Judges 6:12 ESV). Gideon then asked God a question that, sans the particulars, may be on our own lips at times: "Please, my lord, if the LORD is with us, why then has all this happened to us? And where are all his wonderful deeds that our fathers recounted to us, saying, 'Did not the LORD bring us up from Egypt?' But now the LORD has forsaken us" (verse 13 ESV).

God responded by telling Gideon, "Go in this might of yours and save Israel from the hand of Midian; do not I send you?" (verse 14 ESV).

Although God saw Gideon as mighty because He Himself was sending him and would be with him, Gideon saw only his weaknesses. So he responded, "Please Lord, how am I to rescue Israel? Behold, my family is the least [significant] in Manasseh, and I am the youngest (smallest) in my father's house" (Judges 6:15 AMP).

God made it clear that on his own, Gideon may have *appeared* to be weak. But because God would "certainly be with" him, he would "strike down the Midianites as [if they were only] one man" (Judges 6:16 AMP)! Then later, just before Gideon led his fellow Israelites into battle, "the Spirit of the LORD clothed Gideon [and empowered him]" (Judges 6:34 AMP).

When you feel weak and unfit, have faith that God will give you the strength you need just when you need it. For it is by faith that God's people "conquered kingdoms, enforced justice, obtained promises, stopped the mouths of lions, quenched the power of fire, escaped the edge of the sword, were made strong out of weakness, became mighty in war, put foreign armies to flight" (Hebrews 11:33–34 ESV).

"My grace is sufficient for you [My lovingkindness and My mercy are more than enough—always available—regardless of the situation]; for [My] power is being perfected [and is completed and shows itself most effectively] in [your] weakness."
2 CORINTHIANS 12:9–10 AMP

Clothe me, Lord, in Your strength.

Daily Bread

The rich have gloried in their wealth,
And all their wealth has flown. . . .

In her prayer of praise, Hannah is next inspired to sing about how life often turns things upside down, how "those who were full hire themselves out for bread" (1 Samuel 2:5 AMP). Sometimes we ourselves witness this kind of occurrence, seeing once-prosperous people begging for food.

Jesus Himself gives us such an example in His parable of the prodigal son, in which a man had two sons. The younger one came to him, asking to be given his share of the estate that he was supposed to inherit upon the father's death. So the man divided up the estate between his two sons. Days later, the younger son packed up everything he had and traveled to a distant country. There he squandered all his money in reckless living.

Then a famine struck the country in which he was residing. Penniless, the son got a job feeding pigs. In his hunger, he wished he could eat as well as they. But no one would give him any food. Then he finally came to his senses and said to himself, "How many of my father's hired servants have more than enough bread, but I perish here with hunger!" (Luke 15:17 ESV). He determined to go back home. To tell his dad he'd sinned against heaven and against him. And because he was no longer worthy to be called his son, he would ask to be treated like one of the hired hands. So home he went.

The father saw his son while he was still a long way off. So the father ran to meet him, put his arms around him, and, filled with compassion, hugged and kissed him. Just as the son started his spiel, which he'd most likely practiced for days and weeks, the father asked the servants to bring the best robe, ring, and shoes for this son, to kill the fatted calf and prepare a feast. "For this son of mine was [as good as] dead and is alive again; he was lost and has been found" (Luke 15:24 AMP).

Sometimes, like this rich son, we squander the gifts God has given us. Then, when we find ourselves in reduced circumstances, we realize what we have lost, what we have wasted or thrown away. Yet we need not remain there. We, like the prodigal son, can humble ourselves and turn back to God. We can take that long walk home. And in His mercy, God will forgive us, receiving us once again, folding us into His compassionate and loving arms.

May we forever receive our daily bread from the One who is rich in mercy and find the spiritual nourishment we crave.

> *"Father. . .give us each day our daily bread."*
> LUKE 11:2–3 ESV

Father, help me to treasure the spiritual nourishment
You offer, the bread that truly satisfies.

Truly Fed

. . .While toiling, needy, hungry poor,
To affluence have grown.

After reminding us how life may bring the rich to poverty unexpectedly, Hannah takes the opposite tack, saying that sometimes "those who were hungry cease [to hunger]" (1 Samuel 2:5 AMP). This can be true in both the physical and the spiritual sense.

Second Kings 4 tells the story of the poor widow of a prophet. She told Elisha that a creditor had come to take her two sons to be slaves. Elisha asked what she had in the house. She said, "Your servant has nothing in the house except a jar of oil" (2 Kings 4:2 HCSB).

Elisha instructed her to borrow empty containers from all her friends and neighbors and then to shut herself and her sons inside their home and pour oil into all the jars they'd gathered. She kept pouring and pouring oil into the containers until there were no more to fill and the oil stopped flowing.

The widow then went to Elisha, relating all that had happened. He said, "Go sell the oil and pay your debt; you and your sons can live on the rest" (2 Kings 4:7 HCSB).

Yet God doesn't stop at sating our physical hunger. He can also satisfy our spiritual appetite. Although money can be used to purchase food and beverages to fill our refrigerators, freezers, and pantries, no amount of cash will ever fulfill our spiritual cravings. God knows this very well. And only Jesus can satisfy our hunger and thirst for God and His righteousness (Matthew 5:6). Only because of Him are we justified before God the Father. Only He can fill the God-shaped hole within us.

Only after we understand what Jesus did for us, how He died on our behalf so that our sins could be forgiven, washed away, separated from us, making us clean and whole; only after we have spent time with Him, discovering who He truly is and who we truly can be, does our inexplicable spiritual hunger begin to be sated.

As we spend time in God's Word, we begin to get an inkling of our true purpose and realize we don't have to kill ourselves working for material things that never really satisfy. We need not scramble our way to the top, trying to be a success in this world's eyes. Instead, we can discover the love of God, the truth of His Word, the privilege of prayer, the thrill of receiving answers. As we dwell in His presence, we are nurtured by the blessings of His grace, the realization of our salvation, and the gift of His unsurpassed calm.

"Blessed [joyful, nourished by God's goodness] are those who hunger and thirst for righteousness [those who actively seek right standing with God], for they will be [completely] satisfied."
MATTHEW 5:6 AMP

---

*Lord, fill me with Your presence and Word,
and I will hunger no more!*

Discretion

The desolate has sung for joy,
With children by her side;
While she of many sons has failed,
With all her power and pride.

In the next line of Hannah's prayer, she is inspired to prophesy about herself, drawing on imagery from her own life as she sings, "The woman who is childless gives birth to seven, but the woman with many sons pines away" (1 Samuel 2:5 HCSB).

It may be that the once-barren Hannah sees Samuel as a breakthrough birth, paving the way for more children to come. Or perhaps she has had a word of assurance from God that more children are on their way. All we really know is that Hannah envisions fruit in her future.

The number of children Hannah predicts she will have is seven, a number that in the Bible symbolizes perfection or completion, derived from the fact that God created the world in six days and rested on the seventh.

The second part of Hannah's prophecy pertains to one who has already had many sons. This person would *stop* yielding such fruit. This prediction may be pointed directly at Peninnah. *Ellicott's Commentary for English Readers* tells us, "There is a curious Jewish legend which relates how for each boy child that was born to Hannah, two of Peninnah's died." *Matthew Poole's Commentary* suggests the mother of many sons would pine away because "she was now past child-bearing, and impotent for procreation; or because divers of her children, which were her strength and her glory, were dead."*

Regardless of why the mother of many sons would languish, Hannah here makes the point that she and others who were once desolate of children are now on the ascension, while those who have plenty are on the *descension*.

Yet once again, Hannah does not name names. She does not hold herself up as being the woman who was once wronged and is now righted. Nor does she name Peninnah as the mother of many who will pine away. We must credit her once more for her discretion.

The Bible tells us the importance of being discreet. Proverbs 3:21–22 (AMP) says, "Keep sound wisdom and discretion, and they will be life to your soul (your inner self) and a gracious adornment to your neck (your outer self)." Proverbs 2:11 (ESV) tells us, "Discretion will watch over you, understanding will guard you." Proverbs 11:22 (NLT) takes pains to say that "a beautiful woman who lacks discretion is like a gold ring in a pig's snout." Ouch!

No matter what slights we have suffered, no matter what agony we have endured from the words and actions of others, no matter how justified we may think naming names would be, it's better to take the high road. To be a Hannah rather than a Peninnah.

Your words will be an encouragement to those who hear them.
EPHESIANS 4:29 NLT

Help me, Lord, to learn from Hannah to always take the high road.

* The quotations from both *Ellicott's Commentary* (1905) and *Matthew Poole's Commentary* (1685) may be found at https://biblehub.com/commentaries/1_samuel/2-5.htm.

Life and Breath

The breath of God imparteth life;
His power alone can save.

In her next verse, Hannah sings of how "the LORD brings death and gives life" (1 Samuel 2:6 HCSB). How His breath alone can impart life, His power alone can save.

From the very beginning, God's breath was what gave life to humankind: "The LORD God formed [that is, created the body of] man from the dust of the ground, and breathed into his nostrils the breath of life; and the man became a living being [an individual complete in body and spirit]" (Genesis 2:7 AMP).

From this we understand that God alone created (and continues to create) man and woman in His image. That He breathes and continues to breathe His own breath—the source of life—into humankind, transforming earthly dust into body, soul, and spirit.

In Ezekiel 37, as the Lord brings the prophet into a valley full of dry bones, He asks him if those dry bones can live. Ezekiel answers correctly, saying, "O Lord GOD, You know" (verse 3 AMP). Then God, addressing the bones directly, says, "Behold, I will make breath enter you so that you may come to life. I will put sinews on you, make flesh grow back on you, cover you with skin, and I will put breath in you so that you may come alive; and you will know that I am the LORD" (verses 5–6 AMP).

God's breath comes up again when King Belshazzar calls Daniel to interpret the handwriting that appeared on the wall. Daniel explains that he must recognize the power God alone wields, telling the king:

> *"You have praised the gods of silver and gold, of bronze, iron, wood and stone, which do not see or hear or understand. But the God who holds in His hand your breath of life and your ways you have not honored and glorified [but have dishonored and defied]." (Daniel 5:23 AMP)*

Centuries later, the same Greek verb used in the beginning (Genesis 2:7) for "breathed" is used in John 20, when the resurrected Jesus Christ breathed upon His followers and said, "Receive the Holy Spirit" (verse 22 HCSB). It was this new *divine* life that would make His followers new people, new creations. This tells us that the power God has to create, save, and destroy is infinitely greater than the power of any and all other creatures and beings.

God alone has created all that we see and don't see. God alone has gifted us with life and breath. God alone holds us in His hands. May we, like Hannah, acknowledge and praise God and His amazingly creative power.

> *"The God who created the world and everything in it. . . gives to all [people] life and breath and all things."*
> ACTS 17:24–25 AMP

> *Thank You, Lord, for giving me the gift of life and breath. I lift my praise to You alone.*

Life and Death

He brings the strong man down to death;
The feeble from the grave.

Hannah's next verse is about God's power and influence over His people: "He brings some down to the grave but raises others up" (1 Samuel 2:6 NLT). Many scholars believe her words are used figuratively here. That God hurls people down into death and the dangers that lie there, and He also rescues them from it.

We can see an example of this when God allows the rich and prosperous Job to be struck with affliction. Job's test of faith began with the loss of his livestock, servants, and children. Then he himself was stricken with "terrible boils from the sole of his foot to the top of his head" (Job 2:7 HCSB). The extreme discomfort drove Job to sit among ashes and scrape himself with broken pottery. Even then, Job refused to "curse God and die" (Job 2:9 ESV). Instead, he reasoned, "Should we accept only good things from the hand of God and never anything bad?" (Job 2:10 NLT). In the end, "the LORD blessed Job in the second half of his life even more than in the beginning" (Job 42:12 NLT).

In Psalm 30:1–3 (HCSB), David writes about God's work amid his own trials: "You have lifted me up. . . . LORD my God, I cried to You for help, and You healed me. LORD, You brought me up from Sheol." David makes clear that God alone holds in His hands every aspect of life and death as well as prosperity and adversity.

King Hezekiah had his ups and downs as well. When he was near death, the prophet Isaiah gave him a message: "This is what the LORD says: 'Set your affairs in order, for you are going to die' "

(Isaiah 38:1 NLT).

Hezekiah then prayed to God: "Remember, O LORD, how I have always been faithful to you and have served you single-mindedly, always doing what pleases you" (Isaiah 38:3 NLT). He then broke down and cried. In response, God relented, instructing Isaiah to tell Hezekiah, "I have heard your prayer and seen your tears. I will add fifteen years to your life, and I will rescue you and this city" (verses 5–6 NLT).

Besides figurative examples of God bringing some to death and others to life, God's Word provides us with literal ones, such as Elijah raising the son of the widow of Zarephath (1 Kings 17); Elisha raising the son of the Shunammite (2 Kings 4); Jesus raising up a widow's son (Luke 7:11–17), Jairus's daughter (Luke 8:40–56), and Lazarus (John 11); Jesus Himself rising from the dead (Matthew 28; Mark 16; Luke 24); Peter raising Dorcas (Acts 9:36–43); and Paul raising Eutychus (Acts 20:7-12).

Praise the God in whose hands lies the power over life and death, calamity and blessing!

"There is no other god but me! I am the one who kills and gives life."
DEUTERONOMY 32:39 NLT

Whether I live or die, Lord, keep me close to You!

Highs and Lows

The Lord makes poor, and He makes rich.
He casts the nobles down.

H annah next reminds us that the Lord brings poverty and gives wealth; He alone humbles and exalts (1 Samuel 2:7). This aspect of God is shown clearly in the story of Haman and Mordecai.

King Ahasuerus (a.k.a. Xerxes) ruled over 127 provinces from India to Ethiopia. He himself resided in his palace in Susa, the capital of the Persian Empire. It was also there that many displaced Jews resided, one of whom was Mordecai, who was raising his orphaned cousin Esther, whom he'd commanded not to reveal she was a Jew. When the king went looking for a new queen, the beautiful girl was swept up with other young women to become part of the royal harem.

Every day Mordecai would take a walk near the courtyard of the palace where the harem resided so he could learn what was happening to Esther. Eventually Ahasuerus chose her to become his next queen.

Some time later, Mordecai, while sitting at the king's gate, overheard a plot to kill Ahasuerus. Mordecai told Esther, who told Ahasuerus. "When the affair was investigated. . .the men were both hanged on the gallows. And it was recorded in the book of the chronicles in the presence of the king" (Esther 2:23 ESV).

Then the king promoted a man named Haman "over all the other nobles, making him the most powerful official in the empire" (Esther 3:1 NLT). Although all the king's other nobles and officials would bow down to Haman in respect, Mordecai refused. When Haman found out Mordecai was a Jew, he talked the king into signing a decree saying that on a certain day, all the Jews within the king's provinces would be murdered.

When Mordecai discovered the plot, he asked Esther to speak to the king, to beg for mercy for her people. After some fasting and praying, she went to Ahasuerus and invited both him and Haman to one banquet, then another.

Haman was on cloud nine! What honor his king and queen paid by inviting him to not just one but two intimate dinners! After the first banquet, he left the palace full of joy, which quickly deflated when, on his way home, he passed Mordecai, who would not bow down to him. So Haman began building a gallows on which to hang the Jew.

But that night, the king couldn't sleep. So he asked that his chronicles be read to him. Upon hearing them, Ahasuerus realized he'd done nothing to honor Mordecai after he'd saved him from an assassination plot.

The next day, the king had Haman honor Mordecai. Later, Haman himself was hung on the gallows he'd built for the Jew who would not bow. The king then promoted Mordecai to take Haman's position.

Yes, God raises some up and brings others down! May we join Mary, the mother of Jesus, in singing:

"He has toppled the mighty from their thrones and exalted the lowly."
LUKE 1:52 HCSB

Lord, I praise Your power!

Heavenly Treasure

He calls the beggar from the dust
To wear a princely crown.

Hannah's next lyrics remind us it is God alone who "lifts the poor from the dust and the needy from the garbage dump. He sets them among princes, placing them in seats of honor" (1 Samuel 2:8 NLT). This is something Jesus knew very well.

The money-loving Pharisees scoffed at what Jesus was teaching His followers. So Jesus told them, "You like to appear righteous in public, but God knows your hearts. What this world honors is detestable in the sight of God" (Luke 16:15 NLT). Soon after that, Jesus told His listeners the story of the rich man and Lazarus.

A rich man liked to dress in expensive clothes. Every day he lived in the lap of luxury. Yet right outside his gate lay a poor man named Lazarus whose body was covered in sores. He longed for any scraps he might glean from the rich man's table. His only friends were dogs that would come and lick his sores.

One day Lazarus died. The angels carried him to heaven, where he sat beside Abraham. The rich man died too. He was buried and ended up in Hades, the realm of the dead, in torment.

The rich man looked up and across a great chasm. On the other side he saw Lazarus in paradise with Abraham. He yelled out, "Father Abraham, have mercy on me, and send Lazarus so that he may dip the tip of his finger in water and cool my tongue, because I am in severe agony in this flame" (Luke 16:24 AMP).

Abraham reminded the rich man of how, in his lifetime, he had countless good and wonderful things. All the comforts and delights a person could imagine. At the same time, Lazarus suffered greatly, experiencing only discomfort and distress. But now, in paradise, he was receiving comfort while the rich man was in torment.

Then Abraham said, "Besides all this, between us and you [people] a great chasm has been fixed, so that those who want to come over from here to you will not be able, and none may cross over from there to us" (Luke16:26 AMP).

The rich man, now realizing he shouldn't have been so preoccupied with his own comfort, his own gleaning of riches and temporal blessings, but should have reached out to and helped others, asked Abraham to warn his brothers so they wouldn't end up in Hades.

Abraham reminded the rich man that if his brothers wouldn't change their lives and seek God and His righteousness after hearing the scriptures, they wouldn't listen to anyone who rose from the dead (Jesus).

As you live this life, listen to Jesus. He'll make your heart right.

"Where your treasure is, there will your heart be also."
LUKE 12:34 ESV

Show me, Lord, how to build up my treasure in heaven.

The Pillars of the Earth

The pillars of the earth are His;
Immutable they stand;
And all the movements of the world
Are ordered by His hand.

e now come to the line in Hannah's song that gives us the reason God has the power to do all the things mentioned in the preceding verses (1 Samuel 2:4–8). It's because "the pillars of the earth are the LORD's, and on them he has set the world" (verse 8 ESV).

Hebrews 1:10–12 (HCSB) gives us an even better picture of this idea: "In the beginning, Lord, You established the earth, and the heavens are the works of Your hands; they will perish, but You remain. They will all wear out like clothing; You will roll them up like a cloak, and they will be changed like a robe."

The wonder of it is that although the creation that surrounds us may change and wear out, we can count on God remaining—and doing so forever: "But You are the same [forever], and Your years will never end" (Hebrews 1:12 AMP)!

God's power lies in His commands, in His words: "We understand that the worlds (universe, ages) were framed and created [formed, put in order, and equipped for their intended purpose] by the word of God, so that what is seen was not made out of things which are visible" (Hebrews 11:3 AMP). For this planet and its inhabitants, God's power was revealed when He spoke, when He first commanded, "Let there be light" (Genesis 1:3).

Since God created, sustains, and upholds the earth and the universe in which it is set, He can do everything Hannah outlined in the five verses preceding this one. God can break the bows of the mighty and increase the strength of the weak; He can force the rich to work for their dinner and the hungry to become well fed; He can cause the barren woman to bear seven children and the fruitful woman to waste away; He can kill, then bring back to life; He can make the poor rich and the rich poor; He can exalt the lowly and bring down the exalted.

Because God oversees everything He created—including us—we who believe in Him, who follow His Word, have nothing to fear. Because He is good and will do only good, we can know that although we may not understand what is happening in the world, or even in our own lives, God does. He's got a plan. And we are a part of it.

God can use you to bring His plans to fruition. All you need to do is have faith and remember that Jesus is the cornerstone to the foundation God has set. Upon Him you must set your sights and stand.

"It is a precious cornerstone that is safe to build on.
Whoever believes need never be shaken."
ISAIAH 28:16 NLT

Precious Jesus, upon You and Your Word I stand.

Foot Guard

He keeps his saints in all their ways
From every fatal snare.

Hannah next reminds us that God "will guard the feet of his faithful ones" (1 Samuel 2:9 ESV).

But God doesn't just guard our feet. He safeguards our steps. He makes sure we don't trip up or veer off course, keeping His eye on each move we make, ensuring we don't make a wrong turn. David knew this very well, telling the Lord, "You have rescued my soul from death, yes, and my feet from stumbling, so that I may walk before God in the light of life" (Psalm 56:13 AMP).

Another way God keeps us from stumbling is by whispering directions in our ears: "Your Teacher will no longer hide Himself, but your eyes will [constantly] see your Teacher. Your ears will hear a word behind you, 'This is the way, walk in it,' whenever you turn to the right or to the left" (Isaiah 30:20–21 AMP).

An anonymous psalmist reminds us that God sometimes sends His angels to keep us from tripping: "He will command His angels in regard to you, to protect and defend and guard you in all your ways [of obedience and service]. They will lift you up in their hands, so that you do not [even] strike your foot against a stone" (Psalm 91:11–12 AMP).

God guarded the faithful Daniel's steps in a mighty way. King Darius had plans to promote Daniel, but some jealous officials in the king's employ decided to nip that idea in the bud. Yet because Daniel was such a good man, they doubted they could trip him up. They figured that the only way they might be able to file a complaint against him would be "in connection with the law of his God" (Daniel 6:5 ESV).

So these men had the king sign into law the provision that any person who prayed to anyone (divine or human) except the king would be "thrown into the den of lions" (verse 7 NLT).

Sure enough, although Daniel knew about this new law, "he went home and knelt down as usual in his upstairs room. . . . He prayed three times a day, just as he had always done, giving thanks to his God" (verse 10 NLT). The jealous officials found out about it and reported it to the king, and to the king's dismay, Daniel was put into the lions' den.

Fortunately, God was as faithful to Daniel as Daniel was to Him. God sent an angel to shut the mouths of the lions. When Daniel was lifted from the den, not one claw mark could be found on his body.

What God did for Daniel He will do for you. If you trust in Him.

Not a scratch was found on him, for he had trusted in his God.
DANIEL 6:23 NLT

Lord, I pray You would guard my steps, just as You did Daniel's!

Downing the Wicked

And casts the wicked, speechless, down
To darkness and despair.

H annah sings about the contrast between those who are faithful (like Daniel) and those who are not, proclaiming, "He will protect his faithful ones, but the wicked will disappear in darkness. No one will succeed by strength alone" (1 Samuel 2:9 NLT).

Such sentiments are backed up by the book of Job. There, Eliphaz says of God: "He traps the wise in their craftiness so that the plans of the deceptive are quickly brought to an end. They encounter darkness by day, and they grope at noon as if it were night" (5:13–14 HCSB). David agrees, writing in two of his own songs: "Let the wicked be put to shame; let them go silently to Sheol" (Psalm 31:17 ESV); "You, O God, will bring down the wicked to the pit of destruction; men of blood and treachery will not live out half their days" (Psalm 55:23 AMP).

The Israelites experienced the sudden destruction of the wicked during the exodus. To gird up the courage of God's people as they stood trapped between Pharaoh's charioteers and the Red Sea, Moses told them, "Don't be afraid. Stand firm and see the LORD's salvation He will provide for you today; for the Egyptians you see today, you will never see again" (Exodus 14:13 HCSB).

Yes, God proves continually that the wicked will become speechless and be lost to darkness because they rely on their own strength. But the faithful will be guarded because they look to God for their power.

We see this truth vividly played out in the battle between David and Goliath. In the valley of Elah, the men of Israel faced the Philistines. The latter had sent out their champion, a giant named Goliath—who stood nine feet, nine inches, wore 125 pounds of armor, and carried a very heavy sword and spear (1 Samuel 17:4–7)—to taunt God's people.

None of the men of Israel were eager to battle Goliath one-on-one. And then David arrived on the scene. Against the advice of an older brother and Saul, David chose to fight Goliath. Because even though he was just a youth, he told Saul, "Your servant has killed lions and bears; this uncircumcised Philistine will be like one of them, for he has defied the armies of the living God" (1 Samuel 17:36 HCSB). David was sure the God who had rescued him before would do so again. And he was right.

With one smooth stone and his sling, David toppled Goliath. Then he grabbed the fallen giant's sword, killed him, and cut off his head. End of giant.

Never fear, faithful woman of God. The Lord will lift you up and cast down the wicked, never to be seen or heard from again.

"This is the word of the Lord to Zerubbabel: Not by might,
nor by power, but by my Spirit, says the Lord of hosts."
ZECHARIAH 4:6 ESV

Help me, Lord, by Your Spirit, to slay my giants!

Last Refrain

The Lord shall conquer all his foes,
And all the world shall own
The power of His anointed King,
The glory of His throne.

Hannah's song ends in a verse that brings her prayer, praise, and prediction home to her and her listeners as she trills the words, "The adversaries of the LORD will be broken to pieces; He will thunder against them in the heavens, the LORD will judge the ends of the earth; and He will give strength to His king, and will exalt the horn (strength) of His anointed" (1 Samuel 2:10 AMP).

Some Bible scholars think Hannah is predicting the deliverance of Israel from her enemies. In 1 Samuel 7:3 (ESV), Hannah's son would tell the people, "If you are returning to the LORD with all your heart, then put away the foreign gods and the Ashtaroth from among you and direct your heart to the LORD and serve him only, and he will deliver you out of the hand of the Philistines."

After the people complied, Samuel told them to gather at Mizpah and he would pray to the Lord for them. There they admitted they'd sinned against the Lord.

Meanwhile, the Philistine troops, having heard that God's people had gathered together at Mizpah, began advancing. God's people told Samuel not to stop crying out to God for them.

So Samuel offered a lamb as an offering to the Lord. He prayed for His people. And God answered. Just as the Philistines were drawing near to attack, "the LORD thundered with a mighty sound that day against the Philistines and threw them into confusion, and they were defeated before Israel. And the men of Israel went out from Mizpah and pursued the Philistines and struck them, as far as below Beth-car" (1 Samuel 7:10–11 ESV).

To commemorate the event, Samuel set up a stone marker between Mizpah and Shen and called it Ebenezer (which means "stone of help"), saying, "Till now the LORD has helped us" (1 Samuel 7:12 ESV). God's hand was set against the Philistines throughout Samuel's lifetime.

Later on, in 1 Samuel 2:10, Hannah includes another bit of prophecy, this time in regard to the word *king*. At first this title would apply to King Saul, whom her son would anoint as king of Israel (1 Samuel 10:1), then to David (16:13) and many other earthly kings. Ultimately, *king* would apply to Christ, the Messiah, who would rule over not just Israel but the entire world. He would have influence and reign as His message went out to those "in Jerusalem and in all Judea, and Samaria, and even to the ends of the earth" (Acts 1:8 AMP). And today, all those who believe, all those in His realm, continue to find peace and safety.

> *"The Lamb will conquer them because He is*
> *Lord of lords and King of kings."*
> REVELATION 17:14 HCSB

Thank You, Lord Jesus, King of kings, for beating back
the enemy so that Your faithful can live—forever!

Our Salvation, Strength, and Song

Thus Hannah, 'mid the gathered throng,
Poured out her soul to God in song;
And now in peace before the Lord
The household feast with one accord.

I t was just a few years ago that a barren Hannah was pouring out her soul (and wretched tears) to God in prayer. After having done so, she rose in peace and in hope.

And now, having conceived, borne, and weaned Samuel, she has just finished pouring out her soul (and joyful praise) to God in song. This is the sort of behavior that characterizes those who are living a life of sure faith, which is built upon a solid foundation of trust in the Lord.

Hannah, unable to hold in her praise, could not help but sing of all the Lord had done, was doing, and would continue to do. A verse from the song of the prophet Isaiah could have been voiced by Hannah: "Behold, God, my salvation! I will trust and not be afraid, for *the Lord God is my strength and song; yes, He has become my salvation*" (Isaiah 12:2 AMP, emphasis added).

After God had saved His people from the Egyptian pharaoh and the waters of the Red Sea, Moses sang similar words: "I will sing to the Lord, for He has triumphed gloriously; the horse and its rider He has thrown into the sea. *The Lord is my strength and my song, and He has become my salvation*" (Exodus 15:1–2 AMP, emphasis added).

This seems to be a wonderful refrain to keep in our minds to buoy our faith, hope, and joy. But what does it mean?

From the beginning of Isaiah's verse—"Behold, God, my

salvation!"—we are confirming that we have experienced something grand, wondrous, praiseworthy, something we feel urged to tell others. We want them to see what we've seen. To know that God has saved us, providing a way out of our trouble or heartache. And because He did so once, we know He can and will do it again! This fact—that God has been, is, and will be our salvation—means that from here on out we are going to "trust and not be afraid"!

Why? Because the Lord God is both our strength and the object of our song. *He is our strength* means that He will give us the power to get through anything! *He is our song* means that no matter what is going on in our lives, we still have a reason to sing!

Today and every day, make God your strength and song, and praise Him for being your salvation!

The Lord is my strength and song, and He has become my salvation.
PSALM 118:14 AMP

Yahweh, You truly are my strength. You have saved
me over and over again. Like those who have gone
before me, I cannot help but sing Your praises!

Heart over Head

The sacred rites are o'er. The time
Has come to leave the holy shrine.
Near to the altar Hannah stands
With little Samuel in her hands. . . .

The moment has come. A joy- and feast-filled Hannah is standing near the altar. She is going to leave what she has prepared for God with God—her first and only child, little Samuel.

We know that all children, like Samuel, are a gift from the Lord. And that when we send them out into the world, we are merely giving back to Him what we never wholly possessed to begin with. Yet still we wonder how a once-barren mother could bear to part with her only child.

Yet this is Hannah we're talking about. A woman who was dedicated to God, who understood the vow she had made to Him, and who was certain this gift from Him had never really been hers to keep. And so we can easily imagine that Hannah was a cheerful giver of Samuel. She had already decided in her heart what she would give to God. And as she handed Samuel over to her loving Master, she showed no reluctance, no sign of being under compulsion, but released her son voluntarily (2 Corinthians 9:7).

When we give things to God from our hearts and do so joyfully, we can be assured we will find ourselves more blessed than when we receive. That's a spiritual law first introduced in Deuteronomy 15 when Moses told God's people, "You shall give to him freely, and your heart shall not be grudging when you give to him, because for this the Lord your God will bless you in all your work and in all that you undertake" (verse 10 ESV). Echoes of it are found in Acts 20:35 and in Luke 6:38, where Jesus told His followers, "Give, and it will be given to you. They will pour into your lap a good measure—pressed down, shaken together, and running over [with no space left for more]. For with the standard of measurement you use [when you do good to others], it will be measured to you in return" (Luke 6:38 AMP).

Like Hannah, may we always come from a place of giving. In other words, may we not base what we give on what we hope to get back. There should be no thought of what we might receive in return for our offerings. For giving is a matter of the heart, not merely the head.

Whoever sows sparingly will also reap sparingly, and whoever sows bountifully will also reap bountifully. Each one must give as he has decided in his heart, not reluctantly or under compulsion, for God loves a cheerful giver.
2 CORINTHIANS 9:6–7 ESV

Lord, help me give and give, with no thought of what I may receive in return.

Cord of Connection

. . .And yields him to the high priest's care,
With tender words and fervent prayer.

Before Hannah releases Samuel into Eli's care, she whispers tender words into his ears, prays a fervent heartfelt prayer, and then watches as the high priest leads him away toward the house of God where the boy will now reside.

All mothers know that although the umbilical cord has been severed, there remains a connection that cannot be broken between them and the child they have borne or raised. For that connection is one made and reinforced by the spirit of love.

Only God knows exactly what Hannah said to her child upon parting. But chances are this woman spoke a prayer or two between her gentle words of love.

Perhaps she reminded Samuel of what God had told Jacob: "Behold, I am with you and will keep [careful watch over you and guard] you wherever you may go, and I will. . .not leave you until I have done what I have promised you" (Genesis 28:15 AMP). Or perhaps of what Moses had said to Joshua when Moses knew he would soon be going the way of all flesh: "Be strong and courageous. . . . The LORD is the One who will go before you. He will be with you; He will not leave you or forsake you. Do not be afraid or discouraged" (Deuteronomy 31:7–8 HCSB). Those verses would encourage any child—and any mother!

Just as Hannah whispered reassuring words to her child and prayed over him with passion, today's mothers can do the same. Fortunately, God has given us a larger repertoire of verses from which to choose, many more than Hannah had available to her at the time she parted from Samuel.

Mothers who have trained their children in the ways of God should remind those children to continue to pattern their lives according to His Word, to value it, learn it, love it (2 Timothy 3:14–17). May each one of us remind the children in our lives of Jesus' first and greatest commandment: to love Him and to love each other as we love ourselves (Matthew 22:34–40). May we encourage them with the truth that no matter what challenges they may face, nothing is too hard for God (Jeremiah 32:17, 27). That their lives have a purpose (Ephesians 2:10); that they are to rejoice always, pray constantly, and give thanks for everything (1 Thessalonians 5:16–18); that if they keep their minds on God, trusting Him only, they will find peace (Isaiah 26:3–4).

Each of these passages works to nourish the hearts, minds, souls, and spirits of *all* God's children so that the cord of connection to Him will grow stronger and stronger each time we act out of love.

I, Yahweh your God, hold your right hand and
say to you: Do not fear, I will help you.
ISAIAH 41:13 HCSB

Thank You, Lord, for blessing me with Your words of
courage, strength, and love. In You alone I trust.

Training Up

And Samuel finds a new abode
With Eli in the house of God;
And all the household slowly move
To Ramah, filled with peace and love.

After Hannah had sung her praises to the Lord, partaken of the feast, and said goodbye to Samuel, "Elkanah went home to Ramah, but the boy served the LORD in the presence of Eli the priest" (1 Samuel 2:11 HCSB).

Although we don't know what Samuel did to serve God, biblical scholars suggest he may have read the book of the Law, lit the lamps in the tabernacle, learned to sing praises to God, or perhaps played an instrument. Things a young child would be able to do and do well. And year by year he probably took on more and more responsibilities as Eli taught him how to serve their God and educated him on the history and laws of their people.

The next six verses (the ones that follow this account of Samuel serving the Lord "in the presence of Eli the priest") are about Eli's sons. How they were worthless, corrupt, treating the people's offerings to the Lord with contempt (1 Samuel 2:12–17).

What are we to make of such a contrast between the son of pious Hannah and the sons of the high priest? How can one son turn out so well and two others so poorly?

Sometimes it's hard to understand why some children of faithful parents take the wrong road in life. All parents can do is the best they are capable of, leaving the rest in God's hands. Fortunately, the Bible gives us some guidance, some ideas parents can take to heart in rearing their offspring for service to God.

The first is to start as early as possible to "train up a child in the way he should go; even when he is old he will not depart from it" (Proverbs 22:6 ESV). That means acquainting him with the Word so that it will be in his heart (Deuteronomy 6:6–7); setting a good example in and out of church and prioritizing prayer time and personal devotions (1 Corinthians 11:1); loving the child as God loves her (John 15:12); letting him know that even in the darkest moments, God is with him, shedding a light upon his path (Psalm 119:105); reminding her that no matter how alone she may feel, God is there to take hold of her hand and help her (Isaiah 41:13); telling him to put others before himself and to look out not just for his own interests (Philippians 2:3–4); doing everything without complaining or arguing (Philippians 2:14); and following the Golden Rule (Matthew 7:12).

Again, all of these passages are good reminders to *all* children of God. Who are you more akin to—Samuel or Eli's sons?

"Do to others whatever you would like them to do to you."
MATTHEW 7:12 NLT

Lord, train me up in the way You would have me go.

Remembrance

In Shiloh's course, from year to year,
Elkanah and his house appear.
With joy the pious circle meet,
And worship at the mercy seat.

Every year, Elkanah and his family would travel to Shiloh to present a sacrifice to God. On the way there, Hannah's mind was likely filled with memories of how she, when barren, had shed such bitter tears. How at the tabernacle she had poured out her heart before God, wordlessly praying with such passion that the high priest Eli thought she was drunk.

How, when Eli realized his error, he had blessed her, praying God would grant her petition. How God then planted the joy of assurance that the desire of her heart would be fulfilled. As they traveled, Hannah knew she would be seeing her precious boy, the one she had borne, raised for God, then left at the tabernacle. She must have been imagining how much Samuel would have grown and wondering how he had been faring.

Before Hannah knew it, she was standing at the tabernacle with her beloved son and husband, a memorial reunion of sorts. There the threesome may have begun rejoicing, remembering that Samuel was an answer to prayer, acknowledging God's goodness, power, and love for His people.

God would have us all pitch a place of remembrance, a memorial of sorts, a marker where we can remember all the prayers God has answered, all the ways He has worked in our lives. It could be an actual location, a book listing answers to prayers, or a marker of sorts.

After Jacob woke from his vision of angels ascending and descending a stairway to heaven, he took the stone he had used for a pillow "and set it up as a marker. He poured oil on top of it and named the place Bethel" (Genesis 28:18–19 HCSB), saying, "This stone that I have set up as a marker will be God's house, and I will give to You a tenth of all that You give me" (verse 22 HCSB).

Joshua set up a pile of twelve stones in Gilgal, outside Jericho, to remind the Israelites and their children how "the LORD your God dried up the waters of the Jordan before you until you had crossed over. . . . This is so that all the people of the earth may know that the LORD's hand is mighty, and so that you may always fear the LORD your God" (Joshua 4:23–24 HCSB).

Jesus Himself told us to take bread and wine in remembrance of Him and His new covenant with us (1 Corinthians 11:23–26).

How will you memorialize your answers to prayer so that you too will remember what God has done for you and become even more grateful to Him and more eager to pray?

I will remember the deeds of the LORD.
PSALM 77:11 ESV

Today, Lord, help me build a remembrance
of all You have done for me!

Doorkeepers

For there the youthful Samuel waits,
And ministers at Zion's gates.

While Samuel served God as a boy, one of his duties at the tabernacle (1 Samuel 2:18; 3:1) was to open the doors of the Lord's house in the morning (3:15).

Of course, at the beginning of the world, there was no closed door, no reason for a barrier between God and His human creations. But then the father of lies came along and everything changed. "God drove the man out; and at the east of the Garden of Eden He [permanently] stationed the cherubim and the sword with the flashing blade which turned round and round [in every direction] to protect and guard the way (entrance, access) to the tree of life" (Genesis 3:24 AMP).

Even Moses, although allowed to talk to God as a man speaks with his friend (Exodus 33:11; Numbers 12:7; Deuteronomy 34:10), could not see God's face and live to tell the tale (Exodus 33:20).

Samuel had been well reared in the things of God by his mother, Hannah. He knew the house of the Lord was where she had cried and prayed for his conception and birth. Thus, Samuel could have sung with the psalmists, "A day in Your courts is better than a thousand [anywhere else]; I would rather stand [as a doorkeeper] at the threshold of the house of my God than to live [at ease] in the tents of wickedness" (Psalm 84:10 AMP). Why? Because Samuel, unlike Eli's sons, Phinehas and Hophni (who slept with the women ministering at the temple), had respect for his Lord. He knew who God was, seeing Him as One who would "withhold no good thing from those who do what is right" (Psalm 84:11 NLT).

Samuel saw God as the omnipotent and all-powerful Being who had seen his own mother's tears and heartache. He knew God had recognized his mother as good, one who walked in God's will.

Samuel also knew his mother had committed herself to God and hoped in Him, and as a result she was blessed. Thus, he could address God as this same Being his mother had prayed to, singing, "O LORD of hosts, how blessed and greatly favored is the man who trusts in You [believing in You, relying on You, and committing himself to You with confident hope and expectation]" (Psalm 84:12 AMP, emphasis added; see 1 Samuel 1:11).

Thankfully, we no longer need a doorkeeper to access God. For we have Christ—the way, the truth, and the life—who gives us a path to God. Through Him, we can directly enter God's presence and praise Him there (John 14:6; Hebrews 10:19)!

My soul (my life, my inner self) longs for and greatly desires the courts of the LORD; my heart and my flesh sing for joy to the living God.
PSALM 84:2 AMP

Jesus, I thank You for giving up Your life so that I could enter into God's presence.

Joy of Relationship

How pure the bliss! How great the joy!
As Hannah greets her darling boy. . . .

Hannah was not just a pious follower of God with a great understanding of the power of prayer. She was not just a godly woman and mother who rejoiced in God's presence (1 Samuel 2:2), unafraid of bursting out in song before a crowd of fellow believers. She was also a woman who recognized and reveled in the joy she found in relationships.

What bliss Hannah must have experienced on her yearly visits to Shiloh, when she could finally embrace her boy Samuel and in doing so smell his skin, take in his warmth, feel his breath upon her neck and the thumps of his little heart beating in rhythm with her own. She understood the importance of seeking and reveling in the joy of relationship.

So did Jesus' disciple John. In his letter to a "chosen lady and to her children, whom I love in the truth" (2 John 1:1 NLT), John reminded his readers that "we should love one another" (verse 5 NLT). And that "love means doing what God has commanded us, and he has commanded us to love one another" (verse 6 NLT).

The reason John wrote this letter had to do with *relationship*. Apparently, many "deceivers" had been denying that Jesus Christ came in a real body, with skin, hair, bones, and so on. He warned that those who wander away from Christ's teaching will have "no relationship with God. But anyone who remains in the teaching of Christ has a relationship with both the Father and the Son" (2 John 1:9 NLT). John concluded, "I have much more to say to you, but I don't want to do it with paper and ink. For I hope to visit you soon and talk with you face to face. Then our joy will be complete" (verse 12 NLT).

Few joys are greater than that of seeing someone you love face-to-face. Handwritten letters, emails, texts, telephone conversations, and online meetings can only go so far. No joy compares to holding that person you love, touching him, seeing him face-to-face. And if that person is a fellow believer, your joy is even greater!

Yet we will experience even greater gladness when we meet the Lord face-to-face. We look forward with hope to the day when God will dwell with us. When He will wipe away our tears and "death will no longer exist; grief, crying, and pain will exist no longer, because the previous things have passed away" (Revelation 21:4 HCSB). Until that day, may these words help us along our way:

> *"Until now you have asked for nothing in My name. Ask and you will receive, so that your joy may be complete."*
> JOHN 16:24 HCSB

I praise and thank You, Lord, for the joy
I find in You and those I love! Amen!

Bended Ear

. . .And praises God, who bowed His ear
And heard, and answered all her prayer.

Seeing Samuel again reminded Hannah of what she had been through. For when she was barren and being tortured by Peninnah, she may have lamented to herself, as did the weeping Jeremiah, "My soul is bereft of peace; I have forgotten what happiness is" (Lamentations 3:17 ESV).

Yet while in that state of heartache, Hannah knew just what to do: She would go to God and pour out her sorrows, present herself as a vessel for His use, turn her entire self—heart, mind, body, and soul—over to Him to employ as He saw fit. Then, having gone to Him as her sacred refuge, she walked out of His house brimming with the joy that had eluded her for so long.

Hannah's story is here to remind us that God truly does hear our prayers. That we aren't just talking to ourselves or sending a heartfelt message into a void. No, our prayers are reaching the ears of the almighty God who created, sustains, and moves seen and unseen in this world.

The psalmist exclaimed, "I love the LORD, because He hears [and continues to hear] my voice and my supplications (my pleas, my cries, my specific needs). Because He has inclined His ear to me, therefore I will call on Him as long as I live" (Psalm 116:1–2 AMP).

Still not sure God really does bend His ear to your lips? Here's further proof:

- "In my distress I called upon the LORD; to my God I called.

From his temple he heard my voice, and my cry came to his ears" (2 Samuel 22:7 ESV).

- "The eyes of the LORD watch over those who do right; his ears are open to their cries for help" (Psalm 34:15 NLT).

- "He who planted the ear, does he not hear? He who formed the eye, does he not see?" (Psalm 94:9 ESV).

- "Behold, the LORD's hand is not so short that it cannot save, nor His ear so impaired that it cannot hear" (Isaiah 59:1 AMP).

Try to picture God—the all-loving, all-powerful Lord of creation—actually *bending His ear* so that He can grasp every word you are saying, feel every emotion you are conveying, and understand everything you have left unsaid, unfelt. Try to grasp the size of this grand God and compare Him to your own size. Cling to the confidence that no problem, no worry, no impossible feat is bigger than He is.

Then, when God does answer your prayer —and He will—ask yourself, "What will I give to the LORD [in return] for all His benefits toward me? [How can I repay Him for His precious blessings?]" (Psalm 116:12 AMP). And begin your repayment with praise!

> *"Before they call I will answer; while they are yet speaking I will hear."*
> ISAIAH 65:24 ESV

Lord of all, thank You for bending Your ear to my prayer!

Sowing Character

A little coat the mother wove
From year to year with tender love;
And every thread her fingers spun,
Her thoughts were mingled with her son.

First Samuel 2:19 (MSG) reveals that each year Samuel's "mother would make him a little robe cut to his size and bring it to him when she and her husband came for the annual sacrifice." This may have been Hannah's small way of continuing to contribute to the welfare of her child, caring for and supporting him as he served God in the tabernacle.

Teacher and preacher F. B. Meyer writes:

> *What love and prayer Hannah must have wrought into that little coat! Every stitch was put in with such motherly pride. It was hard to give the boy up, but at least she could do something for him. How nice he would look in it! How proud she was that every year's new one had to be larger! Thus parents still make the clothes that their children wear. The little ones almost unconsciously become arrayed in the character that is constantly being sown before their quick and inquisitive eyes.**

Children's minds are like sponges. Although they sometimes may appear deaf to your words, the way you behave speaks volumes. And if your actions don't support your words or beliefs, kids will take note of it. And they will grow up to become people whose walk belies their talk.

God Himself is a father. And when He noticed His children weren't "getting it," He sent His Son, Jesus, as an example (John 13:15), providing a role model we could imitate.

Jesus showed us how we are to love one another. He taught that we are to care for and serve each other. That we are to let our light shine before others so they can see our good works and give glory to God because of them (Matthew 5:16).

The apostle Paul also knew the power of a good example, writing to church members, "Be imitators of me, as I am of Christ" (1 Corinthians 11:1 ESV). He encouraged Titus, "Show yourself in all respects to be a model of good works" (Titus 2:7 ESV).

And it's not just children for whom we are to be setting a good example. We're to be exemplary role models for *all* people, especially those of our sex in our churches. Older women are to be models of goodness. For then younger women will "know how to love their husbands and children, be virtuous and pure, keep a good house, be good wives" (Titus 2:3–5 MSG).

Each day before your feet hit the floor, ask God to help you walk the talk, to be as Christ was, to set a good example for all. In doing so, you will please God and become a blessing to others.

Follow in [Christ's] steps.
1 PETER 2:21 ESV

Lord, teach me how to walk the talk.

* F. B. Meyer *Bible Commentary* (Wheaton, IL: Tyndale House, 1979), 118.

What She Could

And her warm heart delights to bear
The raiment for her child to wear;
As with Elkanah she resorts
To worship God at Shiloh's courts.

I n Hannah's day, the weaving and manufacture of cloth and the sewing of robes and coats were largely the domain of women. So Hannah did what she could within the role allotted to her as a woman and a mother, each year spending her time lovingly and happily making a little coat for her son.

We can imagine the prayers she stitched into its fabric, perhaps asking God to care for and protect the precious child who was no longer under the protection of her roof, no longer shielded in her arms. And chances are the power of those prayers clung like armor to Samuel when he donned his homemade garment.

Of course, bearing and caring for children will always be a woman's task, just as planting the seed for offspring is a man's task. Yet even to this day, women may find themselves playing other assigned roles, often limited by society in pay, promotions, and other rights, but still doing what they can, where they can, when they can. For women are resourceful, innately capable of finding imaginative ways to do what they can with what they have.

In Mark 14, we read of Jesus stopping in Bethany at the house of Simon the leper. While He was seated at the table, "a woman came with an alabaster jar of pure and expensive fragrant oil of nard. She broke the jar and poured it on His head" (verse 3 HCSB).

Some of the people at the supper were outraged! What a waste!

This expensive oil could have been sold for a year's wages and then given to the poor. "And they began to scold her" (verse 5 HCSB). But Jesus scolded them right back, telling them to stop bothering her. For, said He:

> "She has done a noble thing for Me. You always
> have the poor with you, and you can do what is
> good for them whenever you want, but you do not
> always have Me. She has done what she could;
> she has anointed My body in advance for burial.
> I assure you: Wherever the gospel is proclaimed in
> the whole world, what this woman has done will
> also be told in memory of her." (Mark 14:6–9 HCSB)

Woman, regardless of where you are, what you have, or what limits are upon you, think outside the box (or alabaster jar). Imagine in what ways you might be able to do a noble thing. Not for the fame or the record books. But for Jesus.

Do what you can. And you will be blessed as you bless others.

> Do not withhold good from those to whom it is
> due, when it is in your power to do it.
> PROVERBS 3:27 ESV

> Lord, help me to do good where I'm at,
> when I can, with what I have. In Your name.

Joyful Work

Thus yearly at the temple gate
The Levite and the mother wait.

annah was a model of faithfulness. When she was barren and sorely tried by Peninnah's barbs, Hannah still made the trip to Shiloh; she still went to the Lord and prayed away her sorrows.

Then, after she'd been blessed with a child, Hannah returned to Shiloh bringing her boy, now weaned, to serve God in the tabernacle. And she broke into prayer again, this time singing praises! Hannah met with God and prayed during times of lack and abundance, grief and joy.

And on this annual trip, holding the coat she had newly made for Samuel, Hannah and her husband, Elkanah, waited for their little boy to appear. In *All of the Women of the Bible*, Edith Deen writes: "She was grateful that her son, young though he was, could learn to perform many little duties in the tabernacle—light a candle or hold a dish or run an errand or shut a door. And because he would learn to do these menial tasks joyfully, he would rise in a greater ministry to the Lord."*

Every mother is pleased when her child is able to perform a new task, something harder than he has ever tackled before. Hannah was no exception. And chances are, she instilled within her son a good work ethic. One that would give both him and her joy.

We too need to have a good attitude toward whatever work God puts in our hands. And the Word, of course, gives us guidance in this area.

First off, we are to remember that we were created by God in

Christ to do good works, ones God prepared for us eons ago (Ephesians 2:10). It is these works that will bring glory to His name.

Second, we are not to "get tired of doing what is good. At just the right time we will reap a harvest of blessing if we don't give up. Therefore, whenever we have the opportunity, we should do good to everyone—especially to those in the family of faith" (Galatians 6:9–10 NLT).

Third, we are to "be steadfast, immovable, always excelling in the work of the Lord [always doing your best and doing more than is needed]" (1 Corinthians 15:58 AMP), remembering that what we're doing for God will *never* be wasted, whether we see our endeavors come to fruition or not!

And finally, we are not to be slackers but to work with all our might (Ecclesiastes 9:10), knowing Jesus is the One we're truly serving (Colossians 3:23–24).

May we, like Hannah and Samuel, please Father God by faithfully using our talents and energy working for Him.

> *"Well done, good and faithful slave! You were*
> *faithful over a few things; I will put you in charge*
> *of many things. Share your master's joy!"*
> MATTHEW 25:23 HCSB

> *I happily offer up to You myself and my work*
> *today, Lord. May my labors bring You joy.*

* Edith Deen, *All of the Women of the Bible* (1955; New York: HarperCollins, 1988), 92.

The Faithful

Well pleased, the high priest sees them there
Offering their sacrifice and prayer.
He sees the works which they have done
In offering up their only son
And his parental heart is moved
To bless the friends of God beloved.

Every year Hannah and Elkanah faithfully traveled to Shiloh to offer a sacrifice and a prayer to God, as well as to visit their son Samuel. And every year Eli saw them at the tabernacle, doing their duty in honor of the Lord. Their behavior moved his heart, prompting him to say a benediction over the couple, praying that God would bless them.

Second Samuel 2 makes clear that in Eli's day, there were two parties at the tabernacle of God in Shiloh: the reckless, faithless, sin-loving sector whose chieftains were Hophni and Phinehas; and the righteous, faithful, law-loving followers of God's Word, who were presided over by the weak but God-loving Eli. One group was bent on evil, the other on good; one was a product of darkness, the other light; one would draw nothing but curses, the other blessings. And the Lord knew it was the faithful who would keep the lamp of faith burning.

God—who is continually seeking out those who will stand up *for* Him, not *to* Him—is always looking for those whose hearts are fully committed to Him (2 Chronicles 16:9). For it is the faithful, those who are His—heart, mind, body, and soul—whom He will be able to use to work out His grand plan.

In the days of the judges—when God's people had no king and were doing whatever seemed right in their own eyes (Judges 17:6)—not many people were committed to God. Not even after He gave His people kings (their idea, not His) did His people keep to the straight and narrow way.

Faithlessness continues to hamper God's churches today. That's why daily we must remember that long ago, God gave His people a choice: Follow Him and be blessed, or take another road and be cursed (Deuteronomy 28). God has "set before you life and death, blessing and curse. Therefore choose life. . .loving the LORD your God, obeying his voice and holding fast to him" (Deuteronomy 30:19–20 ESV).

No matter what is going on in the world, your life, or your church, be a faithful follower of God. Stay committed to Jesus. "For every child of God defeats this evil world, and we achieve this victory through our faith. And who can win this battle against the world? Only those who believe that Jesus is the Son of God" (1 John 5:4–5 NLT).

May grace and peace [that special sense of spiritual well-being]
be yours in increasing abundance [as you walk closely with God].
1 PETER 1:2 AMP

Lord, here I am, one of the faithful. Use me as You will.

Blessings Breed Blessings

"Lord God of hosts! Thy blessings shed
Most richly on thy handmaid's head.
May olive plants surround the board
Of Hannah and her loving lord."

Hannah and Elkanah, blessed by the Lord with Samuel, returned that blessing to God, putting their son under Eli's care so he could serve the Lord in the tabernacle. Yet now they were bereft of a child. Hannah had no daughter or son she could attend to at home.

Touched by the couple's faithfulness, Eli's heart was moved to bless Elkanah, asking God to make Hannah fruitful, surrounding her husband's table with more children to replace the one they'd left behind (1 Samuel 2:20).

Such a blessing is found in Psalm 128, a song of ascent that pilgrims sang when on their way to Jerusalem or climbing Mount Zion. It's a song that tells of the blessings for each one who, like Elkanah, "fears the LORD [and worships Him with obedience], who walks in His ways and lives according to His commandments" (Psalm 128:1 AMP). Such a person who worships and obeys the Lord will be "divinely favored" (verse 4 AMP) as follows:

- "You will surely eat what your hands have worked for."

- "You will be happy, and it will go well for you."

- "Your wife will be like a fruitful vine within your house, your sons, like young olive trees around your table" (verses 2–3 HCSB).

The last two verses of the psalm contain two more blessings framed as benedictions: "May the LORD continually bless you" and "May you live to enjoy your grandchildren" (verses 5–6 NLT).

That is quite a list of blessings for the person who is not only right with God but fully committed to Him. And that's what both Elkanah and Hannah were: believers committed enough to pray for, raise, and surrender to the Lord their most precious blessing. And in doing so, they became even more blessed.

Proverbs supports the idea that blessings breed blessings, telling us, "The generous man [is a source of blessing and] shall be prosperous and enriched, and he who waters will himself be watered [reaping the generosity he has sown]" (Proverbs 11:25 AMP). On the other hand, "The people curse him who holds back grain [when the public needs it], but a blessing [from God and man] is upon the head of him who sells it" (verse 26 AMP).

Although it may seem difficult to be right and stay right with God, to obey the commandment with which we are charged—to love the Lord with all our heart, soul, and strength and to love others as ourselves—the blessings that follow are worth it.

Consider how you can bless others today. Then do those things, watching to see how God will bless you in return.

Let us consider how to stir up one another to love and good works.
HEBREWS 10:24 ESV

Show me, Lord, whom You would have me bless today.

The Expectation of God's Supply

"Grant that thy servants' eyes may see
Sons for the loan they've lent to Thee."
The prayer has reached the throne of grace,
And God supplies young Samuel's place.

Every year that Hannah and her husband came to Shiloh to sacrifice to the Lord and bring a new robe for their son Samuel, Eli would bless Elkanah, saying, "May the LORD give you children by this woman in place of the one she asked for which was dedicated to the LORD" (1 Samuel 2:20 AMP).

Eli's prayer not only was answered but affirmed the prophecy Hannah had sung the year she left her boy to serve God (1 Samuel 2:5). For over the years, Hannah's family did increase, for "[the time came when] the LORD visited Hannah, so that she conceived" (1 Samuel 2:21 AMP).

God wants us to have a sense of expectation, a feeling of hope when we come to Him in prayer. He wants us to know that He has plans for us, plans to give us "a future and a hope" (Jeremiah 29:11 ESV). For "the hope of the righteous brings joy" (Proverbs 10:28 ESV). To claim that joy, we are to be a people assured that God will supply our every need (Philippians 4:19). All we have to do is believe, to not doubt in our heart.

After Jesus had spent the afternoon teaching a crowd of five thousand men, plus women and children, about the kingdom of God and healing those who needed healing, His disciples came to Him and suggested He tell the people to go away. After all, the crowd needed food and lodging, and they were in an isolated place.

When Jesus suggested they give the people something to eat, His disciples said, "We have no more than five loaves and two fish" (Luke 9:13 ESV). So Jesus took the five loaves and two fish, then "looked up to heaven and said a blessing over them. Then he broke the loaves and gave them to the disciples to set before the crowd" (verse 16 ESV). In the end, not only were all sated but much food was left over!

When Hannah had been barren, Eli told her to "go in peace; and may the God of Israel grant your petition that you have asked of Him" (1 Samuel 1:17 AMP). And now Eli was blessing her and Elkanah again. As she had once before, Hannah believed God heard the prayer, the blessing that had come from Eli's lips. And this assurance entered her heart once again.

Be as Hannah. Be assured God does hear your prayers and the blessings others pronounce upon you. Expect and hope for Him to move in your life in an amazing way.

Now faith is the assurance of things hoped for,
the conviction of things not seen.
HEBREWS 11:1 ESV

I come to You, Lord, humbly and hopefully expecting the best.

The Abundance of God's Supply

And Hannah has her rich reward
Of sons and daughters from the Lord.

I n Shiloh, Eli had blessed Hannah's husband, Elkanah, saying, "May the LORD give you children by this woman in place of the one she has given to the LORD" (1 Samuel 2:20 HCSB). Then the couple went home. And "the LORD paid attention to Hannah's need, and she conceived and gave birth to three sons and two daughters" (verse 21 HCSB). And because the couple believed, they received! In place of the one child they had dedicated to the Lord, they received five more!

When we, like Hannah and Elkanah, live with hope in God, believing and expecting that He will indeed answer our prayers, He *always* comes through—and most times gives us more than we dared to hope or imagine. God proves this repeatedly in His Word.

God makes the promise of abundance in Malachi. Through that prophet, the same Lord of Hosts who worked in Hannah's life said, "Bring all the tithes (the tenth) into the storehouse, so that there may be food in My house, and test Me now in this. . .if I will not open for you the windows of heaven and pour out for you [so great] a blessing until there is no more room to receive it" (3:10 AMP).

Yet, again, we must have faith that God will provide. We must look to Him with the expectation that He will not just supply our need but do so abundantly!

In the New Testament story that Luke relates in Acts 3, we find Peter and John going up to the temple to pray. Outside the gate called Beautiful lay a man who had been lame since birth. From that station, the man often asked temple-goers for money.

So when the lame man saw Peter and John about to go into the temple, he asked them for alms. The men stared at him. Then Peter said, "Look at us."

> *And he fixed his attention on them, expecting to receive something from them. But Peter said, "I have no silver and gold, but what I do have I give to you. In the name of Jesus Christ of Nazareth, rise up and walk!" And he took him by the right hand and raised him up, and immediately his feet and ankles were made strong. And leaping up, he stood and began to walk, and entered the temple with them, walking and leaping and praising God. And all the people saw him walking and praising God. (Acts 3:5–9 ESV)*

When you pray, look to God, fix your attention on Him, expecting He will answer your prayers in a way beyond what you could ever ask or imagine.

To him who is able to do far more abundantly than all that we ask or think, according to the power at work within us, to him be glory.
EPHESIANS 3:20–21 ESV

---

*Lord, thank You for answering my prayers
beyond what I dare to hope or imagine.*

Hannah's Gift

The Lord paid attention to Hannah's need, and she conceived
and gave birth to three sons and two daughters. Meanwhile,
the boy Samuel grew up in the presence of the Lord.
1 Samuel 2:21 hcsb

Hannah's personal story (and poem) is now over. But her faith and dedication to God live on in her son Samuel, the miracle she regifted to Him. The mother is revealed through the works her son performed, the prayers he prayed, the faith he demonstrated, and the service he rendered for God and His people.

Except for her yearly trips to the tabernacle in Shiloh where she would have an opportunity to worship God and visit Samuel, Hannah remained at home tending to her other five children. Meanwhile, "the boy Samuel grew in stature and in favor with the Lord and with men" (1 Samuel 2:26 hcsb). About this passage, Edith Deen writes:

> This links the boyhood of Samuel with that of Jesus. It is recorded that when Jesus was twelve He went to the temple at Jerusalem and tarried there. He, too, "increased in wisdom and stature, in favour with God and man" (Luke 2:52).
>
> *Hannah, like Mary, gave her child to God, and after she did, slipped into the background and became immortal through her son.**

Here once again we see Hannah's selflessness and humility. Having given her very self and turned her dearest answer to prayer over to God, she did not insist on power or recognition or accolades. She merely continued to be a follower and worshipper of God, a wife, and a mother, happy in whatever task God placed in her hands.

At the same time, Samuel dedicated his attention and his heart to God. The Bible tells us:

> *Samuel grew; and the LORD was with him and*
> *He let none of his words fail [to be fulfilled]. And*
> *all Israel. . .knew that Samuel was appointed as*
> *a prophet of the LORD. And the LORD. . .revealed*
> *Himself to Samuel in Shiloh. . . . And the word*
> *of [the LORD through] Samuel came to all Israel.*
> *(1 Samuel 3:19–4:1 AMP)*

Yet Samuel was not just a priest and a prophet. He became a judge and military leader. He was an extremely faithful man with many powerful gifts who was much needed in challenging times.

Perhaps you, like Hannah, have a deep yearning in your heart of hearts, a dream you just can't shake, a vision that continues to play upon the screen in your mind. If so, go to God. Ask Him to use you as His vessel, His tool, His instrument. And when the time comes, like Hannah, leave yourself and your answer to prayer in His hands.

> *Moses and Aaron were among his priests; Samuel also called on*
> *his name. They cried to the LORD for help, and he answered them.*
> PSALM 99:6 NLT

Lord, here I am, dream in hand. Use me as You will.

* Edith Deen, *All of the Women of the Bible* (1955; repr., New York: HarperCollins, 1988), 92.

Becoming Hannah, Part 1: Pray

She continued praying in the LORD's presence. . . .
Though her lips were moving, her voice could not be heard.
1 SAMUEL 1:12–13 HCSB

Hannah has taught us many things. But one of the two main ideas her story impresses upon us is that to have a productive and intimate relationship with God, we are to be women of prayer.

That means we are, like Hannah, to *pray with faith*, "with no doubting, for the one who doubts is like a wave of the sea that is driven and tossed by the wind" (James 1:6 ESV). At the same time, we're not to "worry about anything; instead, *pray about everything*" (Philippians 4:6 NLT, emphasis added).

As we pray about everything, we're to do so *in accordance with God's will*, confident that "whenever we ask anything according to His will, *He hears us*. And if we know that He hears whatever we ask, we know that we have what we have asked Him for" (1 John 5:14–15 HCSB, emphasis added; see also Matthew 21:21–22).

No matter how wrong things are going in our lives, we are to "keep on praying" (Romans 12:12 NLT). *All the time*—when we're suffering, cheerful, sick, and have sinned (James 5:13–18). Why? Because "the prayer of a person living right with God is something powerful to be reckoned with" (James 5:16 MSG).

When you pray, you're to "go into your room and shut the door and pray to your Father who is in secret. And your Father who sees in secret will reward you" (Matthew 6:6 ESV). As you do so, know that God will hear your voice (Psalm 55:17). And if you have trouble finding words, remember that "the Holy Spirit prays for us with groanings that cannot be expressed in words. And the Father who knows all hearts knows what the Spirit is saying, for the Spirit pleads for us believers in harmony with God's own will" (Romans 8:26–27 NLT).

When it comes to prayer, *be persistent.* "Ask and keep on asking, and it will be given to you; seek and keep on seeking, and you will find; knock and keep on knocking, and the door will be opened to you" (Luke 11:9 AMP). Continually "devote yourselves to prayer with an alert mind and a thankful heart. . . . Tell God what you need, and *thank him for all he has done*" (Colossians 4:2; Philippians 4:6 NLT, emphasis added).

And if an Eli or some other person comes your way and supports your request to God with a benediction or blessing (1 Samuel 1:17), accept their affirmation (Matthew 18:19–20). Allow their amen to strengthen your faith.

Pray like Hannah. A woman who poured out her heart to God and was blessed because of it.

> *Trust in him at all times. Pour out your heart to him, for God is our refuge.*
> PSALM 62:8 NLT

Lord, help me become more effective in prayer.

Becoming Hannah, Part 2: Learn to Let Go

The woman went on her way and ate, and her face was no longer sad.
1 SAMUEL 1:18 AMP

Hannah not only teaches us how to pray. She shows us what is gained by letting go.

Hannah was a woman with an unfulfilled desire. She, barren in womb, longed for a child, one she could give back to God. Yet year after year, she failed to conceive, much to the satisfaction of the fruitful Peninnah, who continually tormented our heroine.

Elkanah, who loved Hannah, would give her an extra portion of the sacrificial meat whenever they went to Shiloh to worship the Lord. Seeing how much he favored Hannah made Peninnah even more verbally vicious, prompting her to provoke Hannah "bitterly, to irritate and embarrass her, because the LORD had left her childless" (1 Samuel 1:6 AMP).

During one trip to Shiloh, Hannah, tearful and despondent, unable to swallow her double portion of meat, rose from the feast table and went to the tent of the Lord. There, "Hannah. . .greatly distressed. . .prayed to the LORD and wept in anguish" (1:10 AMP). There Hannah released to God her sorrow. She placed upon Him her desire for a child, her sadness, her distress over her adversary's words. Finally, she offered up her body to be used as His vessel, for His purposes.

As Hannah drew herself up from prayer, she was a new woman.

One filled with the expectant hope that her prayers would be answered. And when they were, when she conceived, birthed, and weaned Samuel, she came back to her place of worship and released to God not only the gift with which He had blessed her—her dear son, Samuel—but a song of praise.

In letting go of all these things in prayer and praise, we see that Hannah gained much in return. For in releasing her desire to God, she saw it fulfilled. In releasing her barrenness to His care, she became fruitful. In releasing her sorrow, she "no longer looked despondent" (1:18 HCSB). In releasing the hurt from Peninnah's words, Hannah received God's balm of sympathy. In releasing her expectations, she received her heart's desire. And in gifting God with her body as a vessel for His use, she became His instrument. Finally, in releasing her son to God, she was overcome with joy, prompting her to praise God. And God blessed her with continuing fruitfulness.

God has already proclaimed release to all spiritual and physical captives (Isaiah 61:1). So release all to Him. Offer yourself up as a vessel for His use. And He will more than bless you in return.

> *Cast your burden on the LORD [release it] and He*
> *will sustain and uphold you; He will never allow*
> *the righteous to be shaken (slip, fall, fail).*
> PSALM 55:22 AMP

I release all I am, have, and desire to You, Lord. Use me as You will.

Scripture Index

Read Through the
Bible in a Year Plan